CONTENTS

CAMBRIDGE LITERATURE

This edition of *The Country Wife* is part of the Cambridge Literature series, and has been specially prepared for students in schools and colleges who are studying the play as part of their English course.

This study edition invites you to think about what happens when you read the play, and it suggests that you are not passively responding to words on the page which have only one agreed interpretation, but that you are actively exploring and making new sense of what you read and act out. Your 'reading' will partly stem from you as an individual, from your own experiences and point of view, and to this extent your interpretation will be distinctively your own. But your reading will also stem from the fact that you belong to a culture and a community, rooted in a particular time and place. So, your understanding may have much in common with that of others in your class or study group.

There is a parallel between the way you read this play and the way it was written. The Resource Notes at the end are devised to help you to investigate the complex nature of the writing and dramatisation process. The Resource Notes begin with the playwright's first ideas and sources of inspiration, move through to the stages of writing, publication and stage production, and end with the play's reception by the audience, reviewers, critics and students. So the general approach to study focuses on five key questions:

Who has written *The Country Wife* and why?

What type of text is it?

How was it produced?

How does it present its subject?

Who reads *The Country Wife*? How do they interpret it?

The text of *The Country Wife* is presented complete and uninterrupted. Some words in the play have been glossed as they may be unfamiliar due to a particular cultural or linguistic significance.

The Resource Notes encourage you to take an active and imaginative approach to studying the play both in and out of the classroom. As well as providing you with information about many aspects of *The Country Wife* they offer a wide choice of activities to work on individually, or in groups. Above all, they give you the chance to explore this ingenious play in a variety of ways: as a reader, an actor, a researcher, a critic, and a writer.

Judith Baxter

INTRODUCTION

The Country Wife is one of the most frequently read and performed examples of a type of drama known as Restoration comedy. The term 'Restoration' refers to the re-establishment of the monarchy in England in 1660 after eighteen years of Puritan rule, mostly under the leadership of Oliver Cromwell. The arrival of the new king, Charles II, after years of fairly comfortable exile in France, brought about widespread social, political and cultural changes, one of which was the re-opening of the theatres which had been closed in 1642. For reasons which will be explored further in the Resource Notes, comedy became the dominant theatrical form of this new era and a highly distinctive comic style evolved.

Undoubtedly, one reason for the appeal of Restoration comedy in general, and *The Country Wife* in particular, to modern audiences is the enduring interest in its major themes – money, marriage and sexual intrigue. The characters of *The Country Wife* reflect the concerns and lifestyles of its first audiences, who lived in or near the locations of the modern West End of London depicted in the play: Covent Garden, St James's Park, Drury Lane. A significant element of the appeal of *The Country Wife* is also its complex yet ingeniously devised plot. You must judge for yourself the validity of the famous reaction to Restoration comedy by literary critic Harley Granville Barker in 1930: 'How could an audience both be clever enough to understand the story and be interested by it when they did?'

Whatever the merits of this remark, it overlooks the striking vivacity of the language found in the drama. Although written in prose, the language is extremely rich and varied, ranging from the highly poetic to the downright vulgar. This is not surprising when you consider that language is also central to what Restoration comedies are about, particularly the way it shapes and is shaped by social relationships. Characters strive to score points off one another through their ability to use language in a society where one of the highest accolades was to be declared a 'wit' – which is the origin of the modern word 'witty'.

The language of *The Country Wife* is certainly far more accessible to a modern reader or audience than, say, the work of Ben Jonson, another playwright and analyst of seventeenth-century London life writing fifty years earlier; it nevertheless may create some difficulty. Therefore, the glossary of this edition is presented adjacent to the text, and is designed not just to help you gain a literal appreciation of meaning, but to encourage you to develop your own responses to the text as you read. In addition, both the interactive glossary and Resource Notes at the back of the book aim to remind you that *The Country Wife* is first and foremost not an historical document, but a living drama script.

Pre-reading activities

All the following activities can be undertaken either individually or in pairs/small groups. They are designed to help you get a feel for the play before you read it, and also to help you to focus more clearly on your own ideas.

✦ *Activity*

1 Find out as much as you can about some or all of the following. If you are working in a group, each member could choose a different topic and give a brief presentation on it.
   - Charles I and Charles II
   - The French Court, 1640–1660
   - The English Civil War
   - The Interregnum
   - Puritanism
   - The Great Fire of London
   - Samuel Pepys and his diary
   - Nell Gwynn and orange-sellers
   - The clothes worn by the rich and fashionable, 1660–1680.

2 The title of the play is *The Country Wife*, which draws attention to one of its main sources of comedy – what supposedly sophisticated city dwellers think of the rural way of life. Imagine that you are an executive of a top company based in the West End or the City of London and you are very keen on your high-powered lifestyle. You have had to spend a few days working in the heart of the countryside and have hated it. Write a letter to a like-minded friend (to be faxed or e-mailed, obviously!) describing your experiences. You should highlight all the prejudices/stereotypical ideas that such a person as the executive might have about country life.

3 Look at the list of characters on page 9. What can you deduce about the characters from their names? Which characters would you expect to be mainly on the receiving end of the play's comedy? What do the names of the characters taken as a whole indicate to you about the kind of play *The Country Wife* is?

Activity during reading

Photocopy a map of present-day Central London (including in particular the Covent Garden area). As you study the play, mark on it the locations mentioned. To get you started, it is worth knowing that *The Country Wife* was first performed at the Theatre Royal, Drury Lane.

A note on stage directions

Exit: one character leaves the stage.
Exeunt: 'they' leave the stage.
Manet: one character remains on stage.
Manent: 'they' remain on stage.

THE PERSONS OF THE PLAY
with a list of the actors who took their parts in the first production

Mr Horner	*Mr Hart*
Mr Harcourt	*Mr Kynaston*
Mr Dorilant	*Mr Lydall*
Mr Pinchwife	*Mr Mohun*
Mr Sparkish	*Mr Haines*
Sir Jaspar Fidget	*Mr Cartwright*
Mrs Margery Pinchwife	*Mrs Boutell*
Mrs Alithea	*Mrs James*
My Lady Fidget	*Mrs Knepp*
Mrs Dainty Fidget	*Mrs Corbett*
Mrs Squeamish	*Mrs Wyatt*
Old Lady Squeamish	*Mrs Rutter*
Waiters, Servants and Attendants	
A Boy	
A Quack	*Mr Shatterell*
Lucy, Alithea's maid	*Mrs Corey*

The Scene: *London*

Prologue

1   *bullies:* street ruffians

5   *The late so baffled scribbler of this day:*
'Scribbler' is an uncomplimentary term for a writer, and here Wycherley is referring to himself and how his earlier play *The Gentleman Dancing Master* was poorly received by the critics.

10   *Castril:* an aggressive character from Ben Jonson's play *The Alchemist*

16   *Bayes:* a name which could stand for any writer (taken from George Villiers, Duke of Buckingham's *The Rehearsal*)

25   *tiring-room:* dressing room (as in the modern word attire)

PROLOGUE,
spoken by Mr Hart

Poets, like cudgelled bullies, never do
At first or second blow submit to you;
But will provoke you still, and ne'er have done,
Till you are weary first with laying on.
The late so baffled scribbler of this day,   5
Though he stands trembling, bids me boldly say,
What we before most plays are used to do,
For poets out of fear first draw on you;
In a fierce prologue the still pit defy
And ere you speak, like Castril, give the lie.   10
But though our Bayes's battles oft I've fought,
And with bruised knuckles their dear conquests bought;
Nay, never yet feared odds upon the stage,
In prologue dare not hector with the age,
But would take quarter from your saving hands,   15
Though Bayes within all yielding countermands,
Says you confederate wits no quarter give,
Therefore his play shan't ask your leave to live.
Well, let the vain rash fop, by huffing so,
Think to obtain the better terms of you;   20
But we the actors humbly will submit,
Now, and at any time, to a full pit;
Nay, often we anticipate your rage,
And murder poets for you on our stage.
We set no guards upon our tiring-room,   25
But when with flying colours there you come,
We patiently, you see, give up to you
Our poets, virgins, nay, our matrons too.

Act I Scene I

Opening Stage direction
Quack: Someone who pretends to have medical knowledge and expertise, but in fact has little or none. In the seventeenth century, medical science was still fairly basic and doctors were not held in anything like the general esteem they are nowadays. The character is an important part of Horner's plan. When you have read up to line 58, consider how the Quack has contributed to the start of the play. What significance do you find in the fact that he is unnamed?

1 Stage direction *(aside):* See page 269 in Resource Notes.

pimp: someone who procures clients for a prostitute and lives off their earnings

1–2 Horner's point is that both quacks and midwives, who supposedly serve the needs of medicine, also help to serve people's sexual needs which are 'natural'.

2 *bawd:* can mean the same as 'pimp'. More commonly, it means the keeper of a brothel, usually female.

7 *eunuch:* in this context, a sexually impotent man – not necessarily the literal meaning of a castrated man

11 *keepers:* keepers of mistresses (not their wives!)

14 *tire-women:* ladies' maids; literally, those who help to dress (attire) their ladies and so know them quite intimately.

16 *Whitehall:* the location of the public rooms of the King's palace, much frequented by those who enjoy gossip and intrigue

22 *the great ones:* a euphemism (a mild version of an offensive word) for syphilis, a particularly virulent sexually transmitted disease

23 *Aniseed Robin:* a well-known hermaphrodite – a person with both male and female sexual organs or of uncertain gender. His sexual activities were considered shocking and bizarre, even by the standards of the Restoration. The Quack's point is that Horner's reputation for impotence will make him as notorious

Act One   Scene One

[*Enter* HORNER, *and* QUACK *following him at a distance.*]

HORNER [*aside*] A quack is as fit for a pimp as a midwife
    for a bawd; they are still but in their way both helpers
    of nature. – Well, my dear doctor, hast thou done
    what I desired?

QUACK I have undone you forever with the women, and   5
    reported you throughout the whole town as bad as an
    eunuch, with as much trouble as if I had made you one
    in earnest.

HORNER But have you told all the midwives you know, the
    orange-wenches at the playhouses, the city husbands,   10
    and old fumbling keepers of this end of the town? For
    they'll be the readiest to report it.

QUACK I have told all the chambermaids, waiting-women,
    tire-women and old women of my acquaintance; nay,
    and whispered it as a secret to 'em, and to the   15
    whisperers of Whitehall; so that you need not doubt,
    'twill spread, and you will be as odious to the
    handsome young women as –

HORNER As the smallpox. Well –

QUACK And to the married women of this end of the town   20
    as –

HORNER As the great ones; nay, as their own husbands.

QUACK And to the city dames as Aniseed Robin of filthy
    and contemptible memory; and they will frighten their
    children with your name, especially their females.   25

HORNER And cry, 'Horner's coming to carry you away.' I
    am only afraid 'twill not be believed. You told 'em
    'twas by an English–French disaster and an
    English–French chirurgeon, who has given me at once,

and unwelcome amongst ladies as one such as Aniseed Robin. Notice how Wycherley would expect his audience to be familiar with this contemporary reference.

28 *English–French disaster and an English–French chirurgeon:* another euphemism for venereal disease. Syphilis was sometimes known as the 'French pox'. Horner's meaning may be that it was caught from an English prostitute and cured by an English doctor (chirurgeon) specialising in such complaints. The first 50 lines or so are full of references to disease. What effect do you find this has?

---

37 *belie 'em t'other way:* The Quack has been hired by young men to declare falsely that they are sexually capable, but never to vouch for their supposed impotence. The Quack is here drawing attention explicitly to the extraordinary nature of Horner's plan.

56 *rooks:* cheats, as in card games. The whole of Horner's speech here (lines 48–58) is important in establishing his credentials as a true 'wit'. What is it about both what Horner says and how he says it that makes him seem convincing?

not only a cure, but an antidote for the future against   30
that damned malady, and that worse distemper, love,
and all other women's evils.

QUACK Your late journey into France has made it the more
credible and your being here a fortnight before you
appeared in public looks as if you apprehended the   35
shame, which I wonder you do not. Well, I have been
hired by young gallants to belie 'em t'other way, but
you are the first would be thought a man unfit for
women.

HORNER Dear Mr Doctor, let vain rogues be contented   40
only to be thought abler men than they are, generally
'tis all the pleasure they have; but mine lies another
way.

QUACK You take, methinks, a very preposterous way to it
and as ridiculous as if we operators in physic should   45
put forth bills to disparage our medicaments, with
hopes to gain customers.

HORNER Doctor, there are quacks in love as well as physic,
who get but the fewer and worse patients for their
boasting; a good name is seldom got by giving it   50
oneself, and women no more than honour are
compassed by bragging. Come, come, doctor, the
wisest lawyer never discovers the merits of his cause
till the trial; the wealthiest man conceals his riches, and
the cunning gamester his play. Shy husbands and   55
keepers, like old rooks, are not to be cheated but by a
new unpractised trick; false friendship will pass now
no more than false dice upon 'em; no, not in the city.
[Enter BOY.]

BOY There are two ladies and a gentleman coming up.
[Exit.]

HORNER A pox! Some unbelieving sisters of my former   60
acquaintance, who, I am afraid, expect their sense

15

63 *formal:* pompous

Stage direction *(Enter Sir Jaspar Fidget, Lady Fidget and Mrs Dainty Fidget):* Wycherley appears to want the Fidget family to be seen as ridiculous. After you have read from lines 63–150 (their exit) think about how you would direct the players to bring out the excesses of their behaviour. How would you establish the contrast with Horner?

66 *occasional:* timely

78 *play the wag with him:* In this sense, torment him. Sir Jaspar has heard the false 'news' that Horner, once so feared by husbands, is now impotent and therefore avoids the company of women. He intends to enjoy this surprising reversal.

88 *(makes horns) ... but I make no more cuckolds, sir:* A cuckold is a husband, sexually deceived by his wife. Horner's making the sign of the horns is a reference to the traditional idea that a cuckold sprouted horns, symbolising how everyone else except him knew that he was being 'fooled'. It is a physical manifestation of his shame.

90 *Mercury, Mercury!:* used by Sir Jaspar as a mild oath, such as 'Goodness gracious!' but carrying a double meaning, as mercury was used in the treatment of syphilis

should be satisfied of the falsity of the report. No –
this formal fool and women!

[*Enter* SIR JASPAR FIDGET, LADY FIDGET *and* MRS
DAINTY FIDGET.]

QUACK His wife and sister.

SIR JASPAR My coach breaking just now before your door,   65
sir, I look upon as an occasional reprimand to me, sir,
for not kissing your hands, sir, since your coming out
of France, sir; and so my disaster, sir, has been my
good fortune, sir; and this is my wife, and sister, sir.

HORNER What then, sir?   70

SIR JASPAR My lady, and sister, sir. – Wife, this is Master
Horner.

LADY FIDGET Master Horner, husband!

SIR JASPAR My lady, my Lady Fidget, sir.

HORNER So, sir.   75

SIR JASPAR Won't you be acquainted with her, sir? [*Aside*]
So the report is true, I find, by his coldness or aversion
to the sex; but I'll play the wag with him. – Pray salute
my wife, my lady, sir.

HORNER I will kiss no man's wife, sir, for him, sir; I have   80
taken my eternal leave, sir, of the sex already, sir.

SIR JASPAR [*aside*] Hah, hah, hah! I'll plague him yet. –
Not know my wife, sir?

HORNER I do know your wife, sir; she's a woman, sir, and
consequently a monster, sir, a greater monster than a   85
husband, sir.

SIR JASPAR A husband! How, sir?

HORNER [*makes horns*] So, sir; but I make no more
cuckolds, sir.

SIR JASPAR Hah, hah, hah! Mercury, Mercury!   90

LADY FIDGET Pray, Sir Jaspar, let us be gone from this rude
fellow.

DAINTY Who, by his breeding, would think he had ever
been in France?

102 *new postures:* pornographic engravings, believed to be in wide circulation on the Continent in the seventeenth century

102–3 *École des Filles:* Semi-pornographic book by Michel Millot, published and subsequently banned in Paris in 1655. Samuel Pepys, the famous diarist, apparently owned a copy and declared it to be, 'the most bawdy, lewd book that ever I saw'.

113–14 *Would you wrong my honour?:* Lady Fidget's first mention of a word of considerable importance in the play – 'honour' (see pages 279–281 in the Resource Notes). In lines 114–119, the word is being used in two quite distinct senses: what are they?

122 *chairs:* sedan chairs, in which passengers were carried by servants

LADY FIDGET Foh, he's but too much a French fellow, such   95
as hate women of quality and virtue for their love to
their husbands, Sir Jaspar; a woman is hated by 'em as
much for loving her husband as for loving their
money. But pray, let's be gone.

HORNER You do well, madam, for I have nothing that you   100
came for; I have brought over not so much as a bawdy
picture, new postures, nor the second part of the *École
des Filles*, nor –

QUACK [*apart to* HORNER] Hold, for shame, sir! What
d'ye mean? You'll ruin yourself forever with the sex –   105

SIR JASPAR Hah, hah, hah, he hates women perfectly, I find.

DAINTY What a pity 'tis he should.

LADY FIDGET Ay, he's a base, rude fellow for't; but
affectation makes not a woman more odious to them
than virtue.   110

HORNER Because your virtue is your greatest affectation
madam.

LADY FIDGET How, you saucy fellow! Would you wrong my
honour?

HORNER If I could.   115

LADY FIDGET How d'ye mean, sir?

SIR JASPAR Hah, hah, hah! No, he can't wrong your
ladyship's honour, upon my honour; he, poor man –
hark you in your ear – a mere eunuch.

LADY FIDGET O filthy French beast, foh, foh! Why do we   120
stay? Let's be gone; I can't endure the sight of him.

SIR JASPAR Stay but till the chairs come; they'll be here
presently.

LADY FIDGET No, no.

SIR JASPAR Nor can I stay longer. 'Tis – let me see, a   125
quarter and a half quarter of a minute past eleven; the
Council will be sat, I must away. Business must be
preferred always before love and ceremony with the
wise, Mr Horner.

150 *foh!:* How do you think this is said?

151–2 *done your business:* ruined yourself

154 *carriage:* behaviour

161 *abuse:* deceive

162 *disabuse:* make them see the truth, or, in modern parlance, 'put them straight'

162–89 *Stay, I'll reckon you up the advantages ... passe partout of the town.:* This is a good example of a set-piece speech designed to reveal Horner's plan to the audience in detail. Dramatically, such moments can be quite tedious. How would you advise Horner to deliver the speech to maintain interest? Think about movement and posture as well as the lines themselves.

HORNER And the impotent, Sir Jaspar.   130

SIR JASPAR Ay, ay, the impotent, Master Horner, hah, ha, ha!

LADY FIDGET What, leave us with a filthy man alone in his lodgings?

SIR JASPAR He's an innocent man now, you know. Pray   135
stay, I'll hasten the chairs to you. – Mr Horner, your
servant; I should be glad to see you at my house. Pray
come and dine with me, and play at cards with my
wife after dinner; you are fit for women at that game
yet, hah, ha! [*Aside*] 'Tis as much a husband's   140
prudence to provide innocent diversion for a wife as to
hinder her unlawful pleasures, and he had better
employ her than let her employ herself. – Farewell.
    [*Exit* SIR JASPAR.]

HORNER Your servant, Sir Jaspar.

LADY FIDGET I will not stay with him, foh!   145

HORNER Nay, madam, I beseech you stay, if it be but to
see I can be as civil to ladies yet as they would desire.

LADY FIDGET No, no, foh, you cannot be civil to ladies.

DAINTY You as civil as ladies would desire?

LADY FIDGET No, no, no, foh, foh, foh!   150
    [*Exeunt* LADY FIDGET *and* DAINTY.]

QUACK Now, I think, I, or you yourself rather, have done
your business with the women.

HORNER Thou art an ass. Don't you see already, upon the
report and my carriage, this grave man of business
leaves his wife in my lodgings, invites me to his house   155
and wife, who before would not be acquainted with
me out of jealousy?

QUACK Nay, by this means you may be the more
acquainted with the husbands, but the less with the
wives.   160

HORNER Let me alone; if I can but abuse the husbands, I'll
soon disabuse the wives. Stay – I'll reckon you up the

163 *stratagem:* plan; another key word in the world of Restoration theatre

165 *duns:* those to whom Horner owes money, of which there are clearly plenty!

172 *chemist:* alchemist, one who seeks the secret of turning base metals into gold

182 *right:* keen to be involved in sexual intrigues, promiscuous

189 *passe partout:* the freedom or licence to go where he pleases, including the bedrooms of ladies

194 *probatum est:* Latin phrase meaning 'it has been tested'. It was often found on prescriptions, hence its appropriateness to the Quack. Horner may also be implying that in sexual matters, nothing is ever truly original.

advantages I am like to have by my stratagem: first, I
shall be rid of all my old acquaintances, the most
insatiable sorts of duns, that invade our lodgings in a   165
morning. And next to the pleasure of making a new
mistress is that of being rid of an old one; and of all
old debts, love, when it comes to be so, is paid the
most unwillingly.

QUACK Well, you may be so rid of your old acquaintances;   170
but how will you get any new ones?

HORNER Doctor, thou wilt never make a good chemist,
thou art so incredulous and impatient. Ask but all the
young fellows of the town if they do not lose more
time, like huntsmen, in starting the game than in   175
running it down; one knows not where to find 'em,
who will or will not. Women of quality are so civil,
you can hardly distinguish love from good breeding
and a man is often mistaken; but now I can be sure,
she that shows an aversion to me loves the sport, as   180
those women that are gone, whom I warrant to be
right. And then the next thing is, your women of
honour, as you call 'em, are only chary of their
reputations, not their persons, and 'tis scandal they
would avoid, not men. Now may I have, by the   185
reputation of an eunuch, the privileges of one and be
seen in a lady's chamber in a morning as early as her
husband, kiss virgins before their parents or lovers and
may be, in short, the *passe partout* of the town. Now,
doctor.   190

QUACK Nay, now you shall be the doctor; and your
process is so new that we do not know but it may
succeed.

HORNER Not so new neither; *probatum est*, doctor.

QUACK Well, I wish you luck and many patients whilst I   195
go to mine.

    [*Exit* QUACK.]

197 Stage direction *(Enter Harcourt and Dorilant to Horner):*
Harcourt and Dorilant, Horner's companions, are classic
examples of a key Restoration character – the gallant. Read
from the entrance (line 197) to Enter Boy (line 258). On this
evidence, what seem to you to be the chief characteristics of
'gallant' behaviour and attitudes?

　　The Boy then announces the imminent arrival of Mr Sparkish,
one who aspires to be a gallant and indeed thinks that he is.
When you have read from lines 258 to 306, identify what the
'true wits' think that Sparkish lacks which prevents him from
being one of their company and therefore deserving of the
name of 'wit'.

199 *raillery:* mockery

203 *orange-wenches:* women selling oranges to the audience.
They were often prostitutes.

203–4 *drunken vizard-mask:* a prostitute, so-called for the
fashionable masks which they wore

222 *beaux garçons:* retired or ageing gallants

[*Enter* HARCOURT *and* DORILANT *to* HORNER.]

HARCOURT Come, your appearance at the play yesterday
has, I hope, hardened you for the future against the
women's contempt and the men's raillery and now
you'll abroad as you were wont.   200

HORNER Did I not bear it bravely?

DORILANT With a most theatrical impudence; nay, more
than the orange-wenches show there or a drunken
vizard-mask or a great-bellied actress; nay, or the most
impudent of creatures, an ill poet; or what is yet more   205
impudent, a secondhand critic.

HORNER But what say the ladies? Have they no pity?

HARCOURT What ladies? The vizard-masks, you know,
never pity a man when all's gone, though in their
service.   210

DORILANT And for the women in the boxes, you'd never
pity them when 'twas in your power.

HARCOURT They say, 'tis pity, but all that deal with
common women should be served so.

DORILANT Nay, I dare swear, they won't admit you to play   215
at cards with them, go to plays with 'em, or do the
little duties which other shadows of men are wont to
do for 'em.

HORNER Who do you call shadows of men?

DORILANT Half-men.   220

HORNER What, boys?

DORILANT Ay, your old boys, old *beaux garçons*, who, like
superannuated stallions, are suffered to run, feed and
whinny with the mares as long as they live, though
they can do nothing else.   225

HORNER Well, a pox on love and wenching! Women serve
but to keep a man from better company; though I can't
enjoy them, I shall you the more. Good fellowship and
friendship are lasting, rational and manly pleasures.

231 *relish:* complement

234 *doze:* confuse

249 *sots:* someone whose brain has become 'intoxicated' so that they are no longer in control of thought, emotion or action

253 *ygad:* corrupted form of the mild oath 'by God'

255 *oil and vinegar:* two elements which are incompatible. They will not mix.

Harcourt For all that, give me some of those pleasures   230
you call effeminate too; they help to relish one another.

Horner They disturb one another.

Harcourt No, mistresses are like books. If you pore upon
them too much, they doze you and make you unfit for
company; but if used discreetly, you are the fitter for   235
conversation by 'em.

Dorilant A mistress should be like a little country retreat
near the town, not to dwell in constantly, but only for
a night and away, to taste the town the better when a
man returns.   240

Horner I tell you, 'tis as hard to be a good fellow, a good
friend and a lover of women, as 'tis to be a good
fellow, a good friend and a lover of money. You
cannot follow both, then choose your side. Wine gives
you liberty, love takes it away.   245

Dorilant Gad, he's in the right on't.

Horner Wine gives you joy; love, grief and tortures,
besides the chirurgeon's. Wine makes us witty; love,
only sots. Wine makes us sleep; love breaks it.

Dorilant By the world, he has reason, Harcourt.   250

Horner Wine makes –

Dorilant Ay, wine makes us – makes us princes; love
makes us beggars, poor rogues, ygad – and wine –

Horner So, there's one converted. – No, no, love and
wine, oil and vinegar.   255

Harcourt I grant it; love will still be uppermost.

Horner Come, for my part I will have only those glorious,
manly pleasures of being very drunk and very slovenly.
       [*Enter* BOY.]

Boy Mr Sparkish is below, sir.
       [*Exit.*]

Harcourt What, my dear friend! A rogue that is fond of   260
me only, I think, for abusing him.

27

269 *offerers:* those who offer or try to be witty

279 *Sir Martin Mar-all:* The foolish hero of John Dryden's comedy of the same name (1667) who serenades his mistress by miming to the performance of his hidden servant. He fails to stop when his servant does and, consequently, is found out.

289 *rooks:* Here, the meaning is fool rather than cheat (as in line 56).

DORILANT No, he can no more think the men laugh at him
than that women jilt him, his opinion of himself is so
good.

HORNER Well, there's another pleasure by drinking I   265
thought not of: I shall lose his acquaintance, because
he cannot drink; and you know 'tis a very hard thing
to be rid of him, for he's one of those nauseous
offerers at wit, who, like the worst fiddlers, run
themselves into all companies.   270

HARCOURT One that, by being in the company of men of
sense, would pass for one.

HORNER And may so to the short-sighted world, as a false
jewel amongst true ones is not discerned at a distance.
His company is as troublesome to us as a cuckold's   275
when you have a mind to his wife's.

HARCOURT No, the rogue will not let us enjoy one another,
but ravishes our conversation, though he signifies no
more to't than Sir Martin Mar-all's gaping and
awkward thrumming upon the lute does to his man's   280
voice and music.

DORILANT And to pass for a wit in town shows himself a
fool every night to us that are guilty of the plot.

HORNER Such wits as he are, to a company of reasonable
men, like rooks to the gamesters, who only fill a room   285
at the table, but are so far from contributing to the
play that they only serve to spoil the fancy of those
that do.

DORILANT Nay, they are used like rooks too, snubbed,
checked and abused; yet the rogues will hang on.   290

HORNER A pox on 'em, and all that force nature and
would be still what she forbids 'em! Affectation is her
greatest monster.

HARCOURT Most men are the contraries to that they would
seem. Your bully, you see, is a coward with a long   295

29

302 *arrantest:* worst. This speech of Horner's highlights another key idea in the play: deception.

305 *fop:* Here, this has the general meaning of 'fool', but the word is used also to describe a type of character such as Sparkish, a man full of his own importance. Sparkish is one of the most colourful and entertaining characters in the play. After you have read the first scene in which he appears (lines 307–382), consider how an actor or director would portray Sparkish. You may find it useful to focus on:
  appearance (dress, hairstyle, physique);
  movement, including posture;
  tone of voice, manner of speech.

321 *signs:* such as were hung over shops to indicate their trade

sword; the little, humbly fawning physician, with his
ebony cane, is he that destroys men.

DORILANT The usurer, a poor rogue possessed of mouldy
bonds and mortgages, and we they call spendthrifts are
only wealthy, who lay out his money upon daily new   300
purchases of pleasure.

HORNER Ay, your arrantest cheat is your trustee or
executor; your jealous man, the greatest cuckold; your
churchman, the greatest atheist; and your noisy, pert
rogue of a wit, the greatest fop, dullest ass and worst   305
company, as you shall see: for here he comes.

[*Enter* SPARKISH *to them.*]

SPARKISH How is't, sparks, how is't? Well, faith, Harry, I
must rally thee a little, ha, ha, ha, upon the report in
town of thee, ha, ha, ha, I can't hold i'faith; shall I
speak?   310

HORNER Yes, but you'll be so bitter then.

SPARKISH Honest Dick and Frank here shall answer for
me, I will not be extreme bitter, by the universe.

HARCOURT We will be bound in ten thousand pound bond,
he shall not be bitter at all.   315

DORILANT Nor sharp, nor sweet.

HORNER What, not downright insipid?

SPARKISH Nay then, since you are so brisk and provoke
me, take what follows. You must know, I was
discoursing and rallying with some ladies yesterday,   320
and they happened to talk of the fine new signs in
town.

HORNER Very fine ladies, I believe.

SPARKISH Said I, 'I know where the best new sign is.'
'Where?' says one of the ladies. 'In Covent Garden,' I   325
replied. Said another, 'In what street?' 'In Russell
Street,' answered I. 'Lord,' says another, 'I'm sure
there was ne'er a fine new sign there yesterday.' 'Yes,

31

332 *crowd:* fiddle, perhaps also an ironic reference to Sparkish's audience for his joke

340 *he's a sign of a man:* He has the outward appearance of a man. Sparkish is implying, with his typical lack of subtlety, that Horner is no longer a 'real' man in the full sexual sense of the word.

355 *exceptious:* annoyed or vexed

359 *wo'not:* will not

but there was,' said I again, 'and it came out of France
and has been there a fortnight.'   330

DORILANT A pox, I can hear no more, prithee.

HORNER No, hear him out; let him tune his crowd a while.

HARCOURT The worst music, the greatest preparation.

SPARKISH Nay, faith, I'll make you laugh. 'It cannot be,'
says a third lady. 'Yes, yes,' quoth I again. Says a   335
fourth lady –

HORNER Look to't, we'll have no more ladies.

SPARKISH No – then mark, mark, now. Said I to the
fourth, 'Did you never see Mr Horner? He lodges in
Russell Street, and he's a sign of a man, you know,   340
since he came out of France.' Heh, hah, he!

HORNER But the devil take me, if thine be the sign of a jest.

SPARKISH With that they all fell a-laughing, till they
bepissed themselves. What, but it does not move you,
methinks? Well, I see one had as good go to law   345
without a witness as break a jest without a laugher on
one's side. Come, come, sparks, but where do we dine?
I have left at Whitehall an earl to dine with you.

DORILANT Why, I thought thou hadst loved a man with a
title better than a suit with a French trimming to't.   350

HARCOURT Go, to him again.

SPARKISH No, sir, a wit to me is the greatest title in the
world.

HORNER But go dine with your earl, sir; he may be
exceptious. We are your friends and will not take it ill   355
to be left, I do assure you.

HARCOURT Nay, faith, he shall go to him.

SPARKISH Nay, pray, gentlemen.

DORILANT We'll thrust you out, if you wo'not. What,
disappoint anybody for us?   360

SPARKISH Nay, dear gentlemen, hear me.

HORNER No, no, sir, by no means; pray go, sir.

SPARKISH Why, dear rogues –

367 *coxcombs:* fools

381 *setting:* sitting. Wycherley here is conveying Sparkish's affected manner of speech.

wits' row: It was the custom for those who considered themselves to be experts at pronouncing judgements on new plays to sit together in the pit. (See page 275 in the Resource Notes.)

382 Stage direction *(Enter to them Mr Pinchwife):* Pinchwife is the last of the male characters to be introduced, the husband of the 'country wife' of the title. When you have read from lines 383–532, think about how Wycherley has presented him as a comic character. Use the same areas to help you focus as for Sparkish (see note on line 305). In addition, what contribution do you feel is made to his characterisation by the use of the aside?

383 *Who have we here? Pinchwife?:* How would Pinchwife react to this greeting? Remember that they are well known to him and he to them.

Dorilant No, no.
   [*They all thrust him out of the room.*]

All Ha, ha, ha!   365
   [SPARKISH *returns.*]

Sparkish But, sparks, pray hear me. What, d'ye think I'll
   eat then with gay, shallow fops and silent coxcombs? I
   think wit as necessary at dinner as a glass of good
   wine, and that's the reason I never have any stomach
   when I eat alone. – Come, but where do we dine?   370

Horner Even where you will.

Sparkish At Chateline's?

Dorilant Yes, if you will.

Sparkish Or at the Cock?

Dorilant Yes, if you please.   375

Sparkish Or at the Dog and Partridge?

Horner Ay, if you have a mind to't, for we shall dine at
   neither.

Sparkish Pshaw, with your fooling we shall lose the new
   play; and I would no more miss seeing a new play the   380
   first day than I would miss setting in the wits' row.
   Therefore I'll go fetch my mistress and away.
      [*Exit* SPARKISH.
      Manent HORNER, HARCOURT, DORILANT.
      Enter to them MR PINCHWIFE.]

Horner Who have we here? Pinchwife?

Pinchwife Gentlemen, your humble servant.

Horner Well, Jack, by the long absence from the town,   385
   the grumness of thy countenance and the slovenliness
   of thy habit, I should give thee joy, should I not, of
   marriage?

Pinchwife [*aside*] Death! Does he know I'm married too? I
   thought to have concealed it from him at least. – My   390
   long stay in the country will excuse my dress and I
   have a suit of law, that brings me up to town, that puts

35

393 *out of humour:* in a bad mood

394 *five thousand pound to lie with my sister:* as a dowry, to marry my sister

396 *cracked title:* Horner's meaning is probably that Sparkish is a bad investment as a future brother-in-law.

409 *Smithfield jade:* a worn-out horse bought at Smithfield market, a place notorious for shady dealing. 'Jade' also meant a promiscuous or disreputable woman, so Horner's simile is apt.

413 *foiled:* injured or below standard in a horse; deflowered or diseased in a woman

414 *clap:* sexually transmitted disease (STD)

415 *cozens:* cheats. Horner's list of those who have caught STD in the country deliberately strays to include supposedly reputable types, such as clerks and chaplains. (See note on Act IV, Scene I, lines 132–135.)

422 *grazier:* one who grazes cattle to fatten them up for sale

423 *silly:* ignorant/naive – the modern meaning is slightly different

426 *breeding:* Harcourt is undoubtedly using two meanings of the word here. What are they?

me out of humour; besides, I must give Sparkish
tomorrow five thousand pound to lie with my sister.

Horner Nay, you country gentlemen, rather than not   395
purchase, will buy anything; and he is a cracked title, if
we may quibble. Well, but am I to give thee joy? I
heard thou wert married.

Pinchwife What then?

Horner Why, the next thing that is to be heard is thou'rt   400
a cuckold.

Pinchwife [*aside*] Insupportable name!

Horner But I did not expect marriage from such a
whoremaster as you, one that knew the town so much
and women so well.   405

Pinchwife Why, I have married no London wife.

Horner Pshaw, that's all one; that grave circumspection in
marrying a country wife is like refusing a deceitful,
pampered Smithfield jade to go and be cheated by a
friend in the country.   410

Pinchwife [*aside*] A pox on him and his simile. – At least
we are a little surer of the breed there, know what her
keeping has been, whether foiled or unsound.

Horner Come, come, I have known a clap gotten in
Wales; and there are cozens, justices, clerks and   415
chaplains in the country, I won't say coachmen. But
she's handsome and young?

Pinchwife [*aside*] I'll answer as I should do. – No, no, she
has no beauty but her youth; no attraction but her
modesty; wholesome, homely and housewifely; that's   420
all.

Dorilant He talks as like a grazier as he looks.

Pinchwife She's too awkward, ill-favoured, and silly to
bring to town.

Harcourt Then methinks you should bring her, to be   425
taught breeding.

428 *private soldiers:*   soldiers of low rank, hence the modern usage of 'private' in the armed forces

432 *ill-favoured:*   lacking sophistication

436–7 *swingeing stomachs:*   huge appetites

446 *moderate portion:*   unexceptional income or fortune

453 *Nine – to my knowledge:*   Horner is pointing out Pinchwife's age – at least 49.

PINCHWIFE To be taught! No, sir! I thank you. Good wives
and private soldiers should be ignorant. [*Aside*] I'll
keep her from your instructions, I warrant you.

HARCOURT [*aside*] The rogue is as jealous as if his wife   430
were not ignorant.

HORNER Why, if she be ill-favoured, there will be less
danger here for you than by leaving her in the country;
we have such variety of dainties that we are seldom
hungry.   435

DORILANT But they have always coarse, constant, swingeing
stomachs in the country.

HARCOURT Foul feeders indeed.

DORILANT And your hospitality is great there.

HARCOURT Open house, every man's welcome.   440

PINCHWIFE So, so, gentlemen.

HORNER But, prithee, why wouldst thou marry her? If she
be ugly, ill-bred and silly, she must be rich then.

PINCHWIFE As rich as if she brought me twenty thousand
pound out of this town, for she'll be as sure not to   445
spend her moderate portion as a London baggage
would be to spend hers, let it be what it would; so 'tis
all one. Then, because she's ugly, she's the likelier to
be my own; and being ill-bred, she'll have
conversation; and since silly and innocent, will not   450
know the difference betwixt a man of one-and-twenty
and one of forty.

HORNER Nine – to my knowledge; but if she be silly, she'll
expect as much from a man of forty-nine as from him
of one-and-twenty. But methinks wit is more necessary   455
than beauty, and I think no young woman ugly that
has it, and no handsome woman agreeable without it.

PINCHWIFE 'Tis my maxim, he's a fool that marries, but
he's a greater that does not marry a fool. What is wit
in a wife good for, but to make a man a cuckold?   460

HORNER Yes, to keep it from his knowledge.

464 *club:*   join together with

478 *gamester:*   gambler. Card playing for money, often with quite high stakes, was a popular pastime amongst both fashionable ladies and gentlemen during the period.

479 *bonds:*   binding financial agreements

penalties: financial forfeits, if debts are not paid on time

485 *whoremaster:*   one who keeps a paid mistress (whore)

487 *box:*   for shaking the dice in a game

494 *keeping:*   'keeping' a woman as a paid mistress

Pinchwife A fool cannot contrive to make her husband a
cuckold.

Horner No, but she'll club with a man that can; and what
is worse, if she cannot make her husband a cuckold,   465
she'll make him jealous and pass for one, and then 'tis
all one.

Pinchwife Well, well, I'll take care for one, my wife shall
make me no cuckold, though she had your help, Mr
Horner; I understand the town, sir.   470

Dorilant [*aside*] His help!

Harcourt [*aside*] He's come newly to town, it seems, and
has not heard how things are with him.

Horner But tell me, has marriage cured thee of whoring,
which it seldom does?   475

Harcourt 'Tis more than age can do.

Horner No, the word is, I'll marry and live honest; but a
marriage vow is like a penitent gamester's oath and
entering into bonds and penalties to stint himself to
such a particular small sum at play for the future,   480
which makes him but the more eager and, not being
able to hold out, loses his money again and his forfeit
to boot.

Dorilant Ay, ay, a gamester will be a gamester whilst his
money lasts, and a whoremaster whilst his vigour.   485

Harcourt Nay, I have known 'em, when they are broke
and can lose no more, keep a-fumbling with the box in
their hands to fool with only and hinder other
gamesters.

Dorilant That had wherewithal to make lusty stakes.   490

Pinchwife Well, gentlemen, you may laugh at me, but you
shall never lie with my wife; I know the town.

Horner But prithee, was not the way you were in better?
Is not keeping better than marriage?

Pinchwife A pox on't! The jades would jilt me; I could   495
never keep a whore to myself.

498–9 *women, as you say, are like soldiers:* What is your view of the way in which women are discussed by the men in Act I of the play?

503 *eighteen-penny place:* the middle gallery of the theatre, frequented both by ordinary citizens and prostitutes. The implication is that Pinchwife has seated his wife where she is unlikely to be seen by the gallants in the pit or boxes below. Unfortunately for him, he has failed!

527 *Hampshire:* English county used in the play as an example of typical rural backwardness, although less than 50 miles from London!

HORNER So, then you only married to keep a whore to
yourself. Well, but let me tell you, women, as you say,
are like soldiers, made constant and loyal by good pay
rather than by oaths and covenants. Therefore I'd   500
advise my friends to keep rather than marry, since too,
I find, by your example, it does not serve one's turn,
for I saw you yesterday in the eighteen-penny place
with a pretty country wench.

PINCHWIFE [aside] How the devil! Did he see my wife then?   505
I sat there that she might not be seen. But she shall
never go to a play again.

HORNER What, dost thou blush at nine-and-forty, for
having been seen with a wench?

DORILANT No, faith, I warrant 'twas his wife, which he   510
seated there out of sight, for he's a cunning rogue and
understands the town.

HARCOURT He blushes. Then 'twas his wife, for men are
now more ashamed to be seen with them in public
than with a wench.   515

PINCHWIFE [aside] Hell and damnation! I'm undone, since
Horner has seen her and they know 'twas she.

HORNER But prithee, was it thy wife? She was exceedingly
pretty; I was in love with her at that distance.

PINCHWIFE You are like never to be nearer to her. Your   520
servant, gentlemen. [Offers to go]

HORNER Nay, prithee stay.

PINCHWIFE I cannot, I will not.

HORNER Come, you shall dine with us.

PINCHWIFE I have dined already.   525

HORNER Come, I know thou hast not. I'll treat thee, dear
rogue; thou shalt spend none of thy Hampshire money
today.

PINCHWIFE [aside] Treat me! So, he uses me already like his
cuckold.   530

HORNER Nay, you shall not go.

534 *Cheapside husband of a Covent Garden wife:* Pinchwife's jealousy is compared to that of a businessman husband from the City for a fashionable wife from the West End.

538–40 The opening Act of the play ends with a triplet (three consecutively rhyming lines). What is the effect of this, and why do you feel it is Horner who says it?

Pinchwife I must, I have business at home.
> [*Exit* PINCHWIFE.]

Harcourt To beat his wife; he's as jealous of her as a
Cheapside husband of a Covent Garden wife.

Horner Why, 'tis as hard to find an old whoremaster   535
without jealousy and the gout, as a young one without
fear or the pox.
As gout in age from pox in youth proceeds,
So wenching past, then jealousy succeeds,
The worst disease that love and wenching breeds.   540
> [*Exeunt.*]

Act II Scene I

This is the audience's first view of Margery Pinchwife, the 'country wife' herself. In this scene she is introduced along with Pinchwife's sister, Alithea, a woman experienced in the ways of London. How do you feel that the contrasts between the two women could be made on stage?

The scene shifts now to Pinchwife's house and, in fact, all but two scenes in the play are set either here or at Horner's lodgings. What does that suggest to you about how the action is structured?

1–2   *Pray, sister, where are the best fields and woods to walk in, in London?:*   This line immediately establishes Margery's naivety about London and would probably have produced an enormous opening laugh from the 'knowing' West End audience during the Restoration.

3–5   *Mulberry Garden ... New Exchange:*   These were all very popular gathering places for sophisticated London society. Mulberry Garden is now the site of Buckingham Palace; St James's Park, near Whitehall, still exists; and the New Exchange, a covered arcade with two long double galleries of fashionable shops, was to the south of the Strand. It was demolished in 1737 (see Act III, Scene II).

20–21   *toused and moused:*   played with, carrying a strong sexual connotation

Act Two   Scene One

[MRS MARGERY PINCHWIFE *and* ALITHEA.
MR PINCHWIFE *peeping behind at the door.*]

Mrs Pinchwife Pray, sister, where are the best fields and
woods to walk in, in London?

Alithea A pretty question! Why, sister, Mulberry Garden
and St James's Park and, for close walks, the New
Exchange.   5

Mrs Pinchwife Pray, sister, tell me why my husband looks
so grum here in town and keeps me up so close and
will not let me go a-walking, nor let me wear my best
gown yesterday.

Alithea Oh, he's jealous, sister.   10

Mrs Pinchwife Jealous? What's that?

Alithea He's afraid you should love another man.

Mrs Pinchwife How should he be afraid of my loving
another man, when he will not let me see any but
himself?   15

Alithea Did he not carry you yesterday to a play?

Mrs Pinchwife Ay, but we sat amongst ugly people; he
would not let me come near the gentry, who sat under
us, so that I could not see 'em. He told me none but
naughty women sat there, whom they toused and   20
moused. But I would have ventured for all that.

Alithea But how did you like the play?

Mrs Pinchwife Indeed, I was a-weary of the play, but I
liked hugeously the actors; they are the goodliest,
properest men, sister!   25

Alithea O, but you must not like the actors, sister.

31 *foot-post:* a carrier of letters (on foot) – rather like a modern postman

39 *bud:* a term of affection

40 *fropish ... nangered:* bad tempered and angered; two examples of Margery's Hampshire dialect which the contemporary London audience would have found amusing.

45 *jill-flirt, gadder, magpie:* a girl of easy morality, a gadabout, and idle chatterer

49 *innocent liberty:* harmless freedom to go where she pleases

54 *lampoon:* a slanderous remark or written document

MRS PINCHWIFE Ay, how should I help it, sister? Pray, sister,
    when my husband comes in, will you ask leave for me
    to go a-walking?

ALITHEA [*aside*] A-walking, hah, ha! Lord, a country   30
    gentlewoman's leisure is the drudgery of a foot-post;
    and she requires as much airing as her husband's
    horses.
       [*Enter* MR PINCHWIFE *to them.*]
    But here comes your husband; I'll ask, though I'm sure
    he'll not grant it.   35

MRS PINCHWIFE He says he won't let me go abroad for fear
    of catching the pox.

ALITHEA Fie! 'The smallpox' you should say.

MRS PINCHWIFE O my dear, dear bud, welcome home! Why
    dost thou look so fropish? Who has nangered thee?   40

PINCHWIFE You're a fool.
      [MRS PINCHWIFE *goes aside and cries.*]

ALITHEA Faith, so she is, for crying for no fault, poor
    tender creature!

PINCHWIFE What, you would have her as impudent as
    yourself, as arrant a jill-flirt, a gadder, a magpie and,   45
    to say all, a mere notorious town-woman?

ALITHEA Brother, you are my only censurer; and the
    honour of your family shall sooner suffer in your wife
    there than in me, though I take the innocent liberty of
    the town.   50

PINCHWIFE Hark you, mistress, do not talk so before my
    wife. The innocent liberty of the town!

ALITHEA Why, pray, who boasts of any intrigue with me?
    What lampoon has made my name notorious? What ill
    women frequent my lodgings? I keep no company with   55
    any women of scandalous reputations.

PINCHWIFE No, you keep the men of scandalous
    reputations company.

64 *town documents:* information about what is to be found in the town

71 *place-house:* main house of a country estate

86–90 *Ay, my dear ... wicked town-life:* A very important aspect of the comedy within this scene is highlighted here. How does it work?

87 *naughty:* wicked. The word has lost most of its original force in modern English.

89 *fiddles:* violins, although it could refer to any common musical instrument in this context

Alithea Where? Would you not have me civil? Answer 'em
in a box at the plays? In the drawing room at Whitehall?   60
In St James's Park? Mulberry Gardens? Or –

Pinchwife Hold, hold! Do not teach my wife where the
men are to be found! I believe she's the worse for your
town documents already. I bid you keep her in
ignorance, as I do.   65

Mrs Pinchwife Indeed, be not angry with her, bud; she will
tell me nothing of the town, though I ask her a
thousand times a day.

Pinchwife Then you are very inquisitive to know, I find!

Mrs Pinchwife Not I, indeed, dear; I hate London. Our   70
place-house in the country is worth a thousand of't;
would I were there again!

Pinchwife So you shall, I warrant. But were you not
talking of plays and players when I came in? [*To*
ALITHEA] You are her encourager in such discourses.   75

Mrs Pinchwife No, indeed, dear; she chid me just now for
liking the playermen.

Pinchwife [*aside*] Nay, if she be so innocent as to own to
me her liking them, there is no hurt in't. – Come, my
poor rogue, but thou lik'st none better than me?   80

Mrs Pinchwife Yes, indeed, but I do; the playermen are
finer folks.

Pinchwife But you love none better than me?

Mrs Pinchwife You are mine own dear bud, and I know
you; I hate a stranger.   85

Pinchwife Ay, my dear, you must love me only and not be
like the naughty town-women, who only hate their
husbands and love every man else, love plays, visits,
fine coaches, fine clothes, fiddles, balls, treats, and so
lead a wicked town-life.   90

Mrs Pinchwife Nay, if to enjoy all these things be a
town-life, London is not so bad a place, dear.

Pinchwife How! If you love me, you must hate London.

94–6 *The fool has forbid me ... upon them himself:* Alithea's speech here and her next two speeches (ll. 108 and 113–114) are asides. What function does she have in this part of the scene? Compare it with Pinchwife's role between lines 151 and 206.

98 *playermen:* actors

104 *Mrs Minx:* Pinchwife's way of referring to his wife's cunning

118–19 How could these lines be delivered to create a comic response? How might an actress use actions/posture to reinforce the words?

ALITHEA [*aside*] The fool has forbid me discovering to her
    the pleasures of the town and he is now setting her   95
    agog upon them himself.

MRS PINCHWIFE But, husband, do the town-women love the
    playermen too?

PINCHWIFE Yes, I warrant you.

MRS PINCHWIFE Ay, I warrant you.   100

PINCHWIFE Why, you do not, I hope?

MRS PINCHWIFE No, no, bud; but why have we no
    playermen in the country?

PINCHWIFE Ha – Mrs Minx, ask me no more to go to a play.

MRS PINCHWIFE Nay, why, love? I did not care for going;   105
    but when you forbid me, you make me, as 'twere,
    desire it.

ALITHEA [*aside*] So 'twill be in other things, I warrant.

MRS PINCHWIFE Pray let me go to a play, dear.

PINCHWIFE Hold your peace, I wo'not.   110

MRS PINCHWIFE Why, love?

PINCHWIFE Why, I'll tell you.

ALITHEA [*aside*] Nay, if he tell her, she'll give him more
    cause to forbid her that place.

MRS PINCHWIFE Pray, why, dear?   115

PINCHWIFE First, you like the actors and the gallants may
    like you.

MRS PINCHWIFE What, a homely country girl? No, bud,
    nobody will like me.

PINCHWIFE I tell you, yes, they may.   120

MRS PINCHWIFE No, no, you jest – I won't believe you, I will
    go.

PINCHWIFE I tell you then that one of the lewdest fellows in
    town, who saw you there, told me he was in love with
    you.   125

MRS PINCHWIFE Indeed! Who, who, pray, who was't?

PINCHWIFE [*aside*] I've gone too far and slipped before I
    was aware. How overjoyed she is!

130 *beholding:* grateful

134 *basilisk:* a mythical creature whose glance was fatal

141 Stage direction *(Enter Sparkish and Harcourt):* The comedy in this sub-scene (ll. 140–340) is heavily dependent upon Harcourt's ability to demonstrate his wit, mainly at the expense of Sparkish, who fails to see the point of Harcourt's numerous ambiguous remarks. The fact that Alithea can see Harcourt's intentions is indicative of her true female 'wit' status, and suggests she and Harcourt are on the same 'wavelength'. What significance do you think this might have? As you read through this section, identify as many precise examples as you can (verbal and physical) of Harcourt's wit.

145 *libertines:* men who habitually lead a sexually immoral life

159 *out of countenance:* not look charming or welcoming

MRS PINCHWIFE Was it any Hampshire gallant, any of our
neighbours? I promise you, I am beholding to him.   130
PINCHWIFE I promise you, you lie, for he would but ruin
you, as he has done hundreds. He has no other love for
women but that; such as he look upon women, like
basilisks, but to destroy 'em.
MRS PINCHWIFE Ay, but if he loves me, why should he ruin   135
me? Answer me to that. Methinks he should not; I
would do him no harm.
ALITHEA Hah, ha, ha!
PINCHWIFE 'Tis very well; but I'll keep him from doing you
any harm, or me either.   140
    [*Enter* SPARKISH *and* HARCOURT.]
But here comes company; get you in, get you in.
MRS PINCHWIFE But pray, husband, is he a pretty gentleman
that loves me?
PINCHWIFE In, baggage, in.
    [*Thrusts her in, shuts the door*]
What, all the lewd libertines of the town brought to   145
my lodging by this easy coxcomb! 'Sdeath, I'll not
suffer it.
SPARKISH Here, Harcourt, do you approve my choice? [*To*
ALITHEA] Dear little rogue, I told you I'd bring you
acquainted with all my friends, the wits, and –   150
    [HARCOURT *salutes her.*]
PINCHWIFE [*aside*] Ay, they shall know her, as well as you
yourself will, I warrant you.
SPARKISH This is one of those, my pretty rogue, that are to
dance at your wedding tomorrow; and him you must
bid welcome ever to what you and I have.   155
PINCHWIFE [*aside*] Monstrous!
SPARKISH Harcourt, how dost thou like her, faith? – Nay,
dear, do not look down; I should hate to have a wife
of mine out of countenance at anything.
PINCHWIFE [*aside*] Wonderful!   160

167 *railleur:* noun – one who engages in witty banter

169 *rally:* verb – to engage in witty banter

176 *ygad:* mild oath – 'By God'

194 *dead to the world:* unable to take part in any of the usual occupations and pastimes of society

SPARKISH Tell me, I say, Harcourt, how dost thou like her? Thou hast stared upon her enough to resolve me.

HARCOURT So infinitely well that I could wish I had a mistress too, that might differ from her in nothing but her love and engagement to you. 165

ALITHEA Sir, Master Sparkish has often told me that his acquaintance were all wits and railleurs and now I find it.

SPARKISH No, by the universe, madam, he does not rally now; you may believe him. I do assure you, he is the 170 honestest, worthiest, true-hearted gentleman – a man of such perfect honour, he would say nothing to a lady he does not mean.

PINCHWIFE [*aside*] Praising another man to his mistress!

HARCOURT Sir, you are so beyond expectation obliging that – 175

SPARKISH Nay, ygad, I am sure you do admire her extremely; I see't in your eyes. – He does admire you, madam. – By the world, don't you?

HARCOURT Yes, above the world, or the most glorious part of it, her whole sex; and till now I never thought I 180 should have envied you, or any man about to marry, but you have the best excuse for marriage I ever knew.

ALITHEA Nay, now, sir, I'm satisfied you are of the society of the wits and railleurs, since you cannot spare your friend, even when he is but too civil to you; but the 185 surest sign is since you are an enemy to marriage, for that, I hear, you hate as much as business or bad wine.

HARCOURT Truly, madam, I never was an enemy to marriage till now, because marriage was never an enemy to me before. 190

ALITHEA But why, sir, is marriage an enemy to you now? Because it robs you of your friend here? For you look upon a friend married as one gone into a monastery, that is dead to the world.

209 *condole:* grieve for

220 *stock blind:* as blind as a lump of wood. But since 'stock' has also come to mean a stupid person, there is a double-edged meaning of stupidly blind.

225 *wants:* lacks

HARCOURT 'Tis indeed because you marry him; I see,   195
madam, you can guess my meaning. I do confess
heartily and openly, I wish it were in my power to
break the match; by heavens I would.

SPARKISH Poor Frank!

ALITHEA Would you be so unkind to me?   200

HARCOURT No, no, 'tis not because I would be unkind to
you.

SPARKISH Poor Frank! No, gad, 'tis only his kindness to
me.

PINCHWIFE [*aside*] Great kindness to you indeed! Insensible   205
fop, let a man make love to his wife to his face!

SPARKISH Come, dear Frank, for all my wife there that
shall be, thou shalt enjoy me sometimes, dear rogue.
By my honour, we men of wit condole for our
deceased brother in marriage as much as for one dead   210
in earnest. I think that was prettily said of me, ha,
Harcourt? But come, Frank, be not melancholy for me.

HARCOURT No, I assure you I am not melancholy for you.

SPARKISH Prithee, Frank, dost think my wife that shall be
there a fine person?   215

HARCOURT I could gaze upon her till I became as blind as
you are.

SPARKISH How, as I am? How?

HARCOURT Because you are a lover and true lovers are
blind, stock blind.   220

SPARKISH True, true; but by the world, she has wit too, as
well as beauty. Go, go with her into a corner and try if
she has wit; talk to her anything; she's bashful before
me.

HARCOURT Indeed, if a woman wants wit in a corner, she   225
has it nowhere.

ALITHEA [*aside to* SPARKISH] Sir, you dispose of me a
little before your time –

59

229 *earnest:* foretaste, guarantee

230–69 Stage direction *(Harcourt courts Alithea aside) ... D'ye hear that?:* During this section Wycherley has, in effect, two separate conversations to be overheard by the audience. What difficulties are presented here in managing the positions and movements of the players? How would you focus attention on the pair of characters who are speaking at any one time? This would have been a key issue in the original Restoration theatre where no special lighting effects were possible.

233 *pander:* one who arranges a sexual liaison for someone else. An equivalent modern expression is 'pimp'.

241 *writings:* marriage contract

249 *wants:* lacks

SPARKISH Nay, nay, madam, let me have an earnest of
    your obedience, or – go, go, madam –   230
      [HARCOURT *courts* ALITHEA *aside.*]
PINCHWIFE How, sir! If you are not concerned for the
    honour of a wife, I am for that of a sister; he shall not
    debauch her. Be a pander to your own wife, bring men
    to her, let 'em make love before your face, thrust 'em
    into a corner together, then leave 'em in private! Is this   235
    your town wit and conduct?
SPARKISH Hah, ha, ha, a silly wise rogue would make one
    laugh more than a stark fool, hah, ha! I shall burst.
    Nay, you shall not disturb 'em; I'll vex thee, by the
    world.   240
      [*Struggles with* PINCHWIFE *to keep him from*
      HARCOURT *and* ALITHEA.]
ALITHEA The writings are drawn, sir, settlements made; 'tis
    too late, sir, and past all revocation.
HARCOURT Then so is my death.
ALITHEA I would not be unjust to him.
HARCOURT Then why to me so?   245
ALITHEA I have no obligation to you.
HARCOURT My love.
ALITHEA I had his before.
HARCOURT You never had it; he wants, you see, jealousy,
    the only infallible sign of it.   250
ALITHEA Love proceeds from esteem; he cannot distrust my
    virtue. Besides, he loves me, or he would not marry me.
HARCOURT Marrying you is no more sign of his love than
    bribing your woman, that he may marry you, is a sign
    of his generosity. Marriage is rather a sign of interest   255
    than love, and he that marries a fortune covets a
    mistress, not loves her. But if you take marriage for a
    sign of love, take it from me immediately.

259 *scruple:* objection

264 *necessity for a cloak:* to hide a pregnancy

272 *cit:* a contemptuous term for an ordinary citizen – not a
gentleman

278 *bubble:* a gullible fool

ALITHEA No, now you have put a scruple in my head; but, in short, sir, to end our dispute, I must marry him, my reputation would suffer in the world else.   260

HARCOURT No, if you do marry him, with your pardon, madam, your reputation suffers in the world and you would be thought in necessity for a cloak.

ALITHEA Nay, now you are rude, sir. – Mr Sparkish, pray   265 come hither, your friend here is very troublesome, and very loving.

HARCOURT [*aside to* ALITHEA] Hold, hold! –

PINCHWIFE D'ye hear that?

SPARKISH Why, d'ye think I'll seem to be jealous, like a   270 country bumpkin?

PINCHWIFE No, rather be a cuckold, like a credulous cit.

HARCOURT Madam, you would not have been so little generous as to have told him.

ALITHEA Yes, since you could be so little generous as to   275 wrong him.

HARCOURT Wrong him! No man can do't, he's beneath an injury; a bubble, a coward, a senseless idiot, a wretch so contemptible to all the world but you that –

ALITHEA Hold, do not rail at him, for since he is like to be   280 my husband, I am resolved to like him. Nay, I think I am obliged to tell him you are not his friend. – Master Sparkish, Master Sparkish.

SPARKISH What, what? – Now, dear rogue, has not she wit?   285

HARCOURT [*speaks surlily*] Not so much as I thought and hoped she had.

ALITHEA Mr Sparkish, do you bring people to rail at you?

HARCOURT Madam –

SPARKISH How! No, but if he does rail at me, 'tis but in   290 jest, I warrant; what we wits do for one another and never take any notice of it.

296 *parts:* intelligence and wit. A modern audience may find this line even funnier than a seventeenth-century one because of the double meaning of 'parts' as genitals.

301–2 *Damned, senseless … jade:* Is this a compliment to Alithea or a criticism? What does it suggest to you about the morality of Harcourt's position in general during the scene?

309–13 *How! Did he disparage my parts? … before my mistress:* Here, Wycherley is parodying heroic posturing, quite common in Restoration society.

318 *person:* appearance

ALITHEA He spoke so scurrilously of you, I had no patience
to hear him; besides, he has been making love to me.

HARCOURT [*aside*] True, damned, telltale woman!   295

SPARKISH Pshaw, to show his parts – we wits rail and
make love often but to show our parts; as we have no
affections, so we have no malice. We –

ALITHEA He said you were a wretch, below an injury.

SPARKISH Pshaw!   300

HARCOURT [*aside*] Damned, senseless, impudent, virtuous
jade! Well, since she won't let me have her, she'll do as
good, she'll make me hate her.

ALITHEA A common bubble.

SPARKISH Pshaw!   305

ALITHEA A coward.

SPARKISH Pshaw, pshaw!

ALITHEA A senseless, drivelling idiot.

SPARKISH How! Did he disparage my parts? Nay, then my
honour's concerned; I can't put up that, sir, by the   310
world. Brother, help me to kill him. [*Aside*] I may
draw now, since we have the odds of him. 'Tis a good
occasion, too, before my mistress –

  [*Offers to draw.*]

ALITHEA Hold, hold!

SPARKISH What, what?   315

ALITHEA [*aside*] I must not let 'em kill the gentleman
neither, for his kindness to me; I am so far from hating
him that I wish my gallant had his person and
understanding. – Nay, if my honour –

SPARKISH I'll be thy death.   320

ALITHEA Hold, hold! Indeed, to tell the truth, the
gentleman said after all that what he spoke was but
out of friendship to you.

SPARKISH How! say I am, I am a fool, that is, no wit, out
of friendship to me?   325

65

339 *trimmings:* clothes

341–4 *Well, go thy ways ... freehold:* The connection between marriage and money referred to here by Pinchwife is a key theme of the play. Note examples of it as you work through the text.

342–3 *come to 'em:* inherit them

349 *civility:* politeness

ALITHEA Yes, to try whether I was concerned enough for
you and made love to me only to be satisfied of my
virtue, for your sake.

HARCOURT [*aside*] Kind, however –

SPARKISH Nay, if it were so, my dear rogue, I ask thee   330
pardon; but why would not you tell me so, faith?

HARCOURT Because I did not think on't, faith.

SPARKISH Come, Horner does not come, Harcourt, let's be
gone to the new play. – Come, madam.

ALITHEA I will not go if you intend to leave me alone in the   335
box and run into the pit, as you use to do.

SPARKISH Pshaw! I'll leave Harcourt with you in the box
to entertain you, and that's as good; if I sat in the box,
I should be thought no judge but of trimmings. –
Come away, Harcourt, lead her down.   340

[*Exeunt* SPARKISH, HARCOURT *and* ALITHEA.]

PINCHWIFE Well, go thy ways, for the flower of the true
town fops, such as spend their estates before they come
to 'em and are cuckolds before they're married. But let
me go look to my own freehold. – How! –

[*Enter* MY LADY FIDGET, MRS DAINTY FIDGET *and*
MRS SQUEAMISH.]

LADY FIDGET Your servant, sir; where is your lady? We are   345
come to wait upon her to the new play.

PINCHWIFE New play!

LADY FIDGET And my husband will wait upon you presently.

PINCHWIFE [*aside*] Damn your civility. – Madam, by no
means; I will not see Sir Jaspar here till I have waited   350
upon him at home; nor shall my wife see you till she
has waited upon your ladyship at your lodgings.

LADY FIDGET Now we are here, sir –

PINCHWIFE No, madam.

DAINTY Pray, let us see her.   355

SQUEAMISH We will not stir till we see her.

PINCHWIFE [*aside*] A pox on you all!

364 *smallpox:* This acutely infectious disease, which results in eruptions upon the skin, was particularly virulent at the time and could be fatal as well as disfiguring. The reference here, even in a comic context, continues the disease imagery established in the opening scene of the play.

375 Stage direction *(Exit Pinchwife):* Here we see three 'women of quality' in conversation together with no men present. When you have read this quite demanding section, consider:
– what the ladies are complaining about;
– what they mean by the word 'honour';
– what you think of their moral position in general (note especially lines 428–429 '… the crime's the less when 'tis not known');
– the effect of presenting them to the audience in this way;
– how their behaviour differs when there are men present.

384 *in keeping little playhouse creatures:* There is a Restoration joke here. The actress playing the part of Mrs Squeamish may well have been such a 'little playhouse creature' herself.

[*Goes to the door, and returns.*]

– She has locked the door and is gone abroad.

Lady Fidget No, you have locked the door and she's within.

Dainty They told us below she was here.   360

Pinchwife [*aside*] Will nothing do? – Well, it must out
then. To tell you the truth, ladies, which I was afraid
to let you know before, lest it might endanger your
lives, my wife has just now the smallpox come out
upon her. Do not be frightened but pray, be gone,   365
ladies; you shall not stay here in danger of your lives.
Pray get you gone, ladies.

Lady Fidget No, no, we have all had 'em.

Squeamish Alack, alack.

Dainty Come, come, we must see how it goes with her; I   370
understand the disease.

Lady Fidget Come.

Pinchwife [*aside*] Well, there is no being too hard for
women at their own weapon, lying; therefore I'll quit
the field.   375

[*Exit* PINCHWIFE.]

Squeamish Here's an example of jealousy.

Lady Fidget Indeed, as the world goes, I wonder there are
no more jealous, since wives are so neglected.

Dainty Pshaw, as the world goes, to what end should they
be jealous?   380

Lady Fidget Foh, 'tis a nasty world.

Squeamish That men of parts, great acquaintance and
quality should take up with and spend themselves and
fortunes in keeping little playhouse creatures, foh!

Lady Fidget Nay, that women of understanding, great   385
acquaintance and good quality should fall a-keeping
too of little creatures, foh!

Squeamish Why, 'tis the men of quality's fault; they never
visit women of honour and reputation, as they used to
do and have not so much as common civility for ladies   390

69

391 *indifferency:* lack of interest or concern. The modern version of the noun is 'indifference'.

394 *Methinks birth, birth …:* What effect is created by the repetition of 'birth' here?

405–7 The tone of Dainty's remark is sarcastic.

409–11 *To report … a person:* How has the comic effect been created here?

422–3 *Whither shall we ramble?:* What are we talking about? ie let's get back to a more proper subject.

423 *continent:* restrained, controlled

of our rank, but use us with the same indifferency and
ill-breeding as if we were all married to 'em.

LADY FIDGET She says true; 'tis an arrant shame women of
quality should be so slighted. Methinks birth, birth
should go for something. I have known men admired,   395
courted and followed for their titles only.

SQUEAMISH Ay, one would think men of honour should not
love, no more than marry, out of their own rank.

DAINTY Fie, fie upon 'em! They are come to think
crossbreeding for themselves best, as well as for their   400
dogs and horses.

LADY FIDGET They are dogs and horses for't.

SQUEAMISH One would think, if not for love, for vanity a
little.

DAINTY Nay, they do satisfy their vanity upon us   405
sometimes and are kind to us in their report: tell all the
world they lie with us.

LADY FIDGET Damned rascals! That we should be only
wronged by 'em! To report a man has had a person,
when he has not had a person, is the greatest wrong in   410
the whole world that can be done to a person.

SQUEAMISH Well, 'tis an arrant shame noble persons should
be so wronged and neglected.

LADY FIDGET But still 'tis an arranter shame for a noble
person to neglect her own honour and defame her own   415
noble person with little inconsiderable fellows, foh!

DAINTY I suppose the crime against our honour is the same
with a man of quality as with another.

LADY FIDGET How! No, sure, the man of quality is likest one's
husband and therefore the fault should be the less.   420

DAINTY But then the pleasure should be the less.

LADY FIDGET Fie, fie, fie, for shame, sister! Whither shall we
ramble? Be continent in your discourse, or I shall hate
you.

426 *quality:* rank in society

434–5 Dainty's aside to Squeamish indicates her suspicions that Lady Fidget has a particular lover in mind. It also suggests that despite the ladies' apparent openness on the subject of men's infidelity, each is examining the others' words and actions for clues about current intrigues. They are all potential rivals!

451–2 *Mr Tattle or Master Limberham:* names of harmless old gallants, 'beaux garçons' as mentioned in Act I, Scene I, line 222

DAINTY Besides, an intrigue is so much the more notorious   425
    for the man's quality.

SQUEAMISH 'Tis true, nobody takes notice of a private man
    and therefore with him 'tis more secret, and the crime's
    the less when 'tis not known.

LADY FIDGET You say true; i'faith, I think you are in the right   430
    on't. 'Tis not an injury to a husband till it be an injury to
    our honours; so that a woman of honour loses no
    honour with a private person; and to say truth –

DAINTY [*apart to* SQUEAMISH] So, the little fellow is
    grown a private person – with her –   435

LADY FIDGET But still my dear, dear honour.

    [*Enter* SIR JASPAR, HORNER, DORILANT.]

SIR JASPAR Ay, my dear, dear of honour, thou hast still so
    much honour in thy mouth –

HORNER [*aside*] That she has none elsewhere.

LADY FIDGET Oh, what d'ye mean to bring in these upon us?   440

DAINTY Foh, these are as bad as wits.

SQUEAMISH Foh!

LADY FIDGET Let us leave the room.

SIR JASPAR Stay, stay; faith, to tell you the naked truth –

LADY FIDGET Fie, Sir Jaspar, do not use that word 'naked'.   445

SIR JASPAR Well, well, in short, I have business at
    Whitehall and cannot go to the play with you,
    therefore would have you go –

LADY FIDGET With those two to a play?

SIR JASPAR No, not with t'other but with Mr Horner; there   450
    can be no more scandal to go with him than with Mr
    Tattle or Master Limberham.

LADY FIDGET With that nasty fellow! No – no!

SIR JASPAR Nay, prithee, dear, hear me.

    [*Whispers to* LADY FIDGET.]

HORNER Ladies –   455

    [HORNER, DORILANT *drawing near* SQUEAMISH
    and DAINTY.]

73

458 *herd:* consort with, keep the company of. The animal image conveys Dainty's low opinion of such behaviour.

464-9 *Why, these are pretenders to honour ... great honour as quality:* Notice how quickly and perceptively Horner exposes the hypocrisy of the ladies. Look out for further examples of his wit in this scene, including the famous 'set-piece' speech comparing women and spaniels (lines 506-512).

467 *arithmetical:* fussily over-precise

Dainty Stand off.

Squeamish Do not approach us.

Dainty You herd with the wits, you are obscenity all over.

Squeamish And I would as soon look upon a picture of Adam and Eve, without fig leaves, as any of you, if I could help it; therefore keep off and do not make us sick. 460

Dorilant What a devil are these?

Horner Why, these are pretenders to honour, as critics to wit, only by censuring others; and as every raw, peevish, out-of-humoured, affected, dull, tea-drinking, arithmetical fop sets up for a wit by railing at men of sense, so these for honour by railing at the Court and ladies of as great honour as quality. 465

Sir Jaspar Come, Mr Horner, I must desire you to go with these ladies to the play, sir. 470

Horner I, sir!

Sir Jaspar Ay, ay, come, sir.

Horner I must beg your pardon, sir, and theirs; I will not be seen in women's company in public again for the world. 475

Sir Jaspar Ha, ha, strange aversion!

Squeamish No, he's for women's company in private.

Sir Jaspar He – poor man – he! Hah, ha, ha!

Dainty 'Tis a greater shame amongst lewd fellows to be seen in virtuous women's company than for the women to be seen with them. 480

Horner Indeed, madam, the time was I only hated virtuous women, but now I hate the other too; I beg your pardon, ladies. 485

Lady Fidget You are very obliging, sir, because we would not be troubled with you.

Sir Jaspar In sober sadness, he shall go.

Dorilant Nay, if he wo'not, I am ready to wait upon the ladies; and I think I am the fitter man. 490

491–2 *Master Horner is a privileged man:*   Sir Jaspar ironically exults in Horner's 'misfortune' but the extent of the success of Horner's plan so far is shown by Sir Jaspar using the very word Horner himself chose when describing his idea to the Quack – 'privileged'.

500 *Great Turk's seraglio:*   the harem of the Turkish sultan, the place most commonly associated with eunuchs

501 *ombre:*   one of the most popular card games amongst the fashionable set. Dorilant may also be suggesting a bawdy pun on hombre ('hombre' is the Spanish word for 'man'). He doesn't want to play at being a man.

516 *mortified:*   decayed

516–17 *French wether:*   a castrated ram

523 *drolling:*   ridiculous, clown-like

Sir Jaspar You, sir? No, I thank you for that – Master
Horner is a privileged man amongst the virtuous
ladies; 'twill be a great while before you are so; heh,
he, he! He's my wife's gallant, heh, he, he! No, pray
withdraw, sir, for as I take it, the virtuous ladies have   495
no business with you.

Dorilant And I am sure he can have none with them. 'Tis
strange a man can't come amongst virtuous women
now but upon the same terms as men are admitted into
the Great Turk's seraglio; but heavens keep me from   500
being an ombre player with 'em! But where is
Pinchwife?
    [*Exit* DORILANT.]

Sir Jaspar Come, come, man; what, avoid the sweet
society of womankind? that sweet, soft, gentle, tame,
noble creature, woman, made for man's companion –   505

Horner So is that soft, gentle, tame and more noble
creature a spaniel, and has all their tricks: can fawn, lie
down, suffer beating and fawn the more; barks at your
friends when they come to see you; makes your bed
hard; gives you fleas, and the mange sometimes. And   510
all the difference is, the spaniel's the more faithful
animal and fawns but upon one master.

Sir Jaspar Heh, he, he!

Squeamish Oh, the rude beast!

Dainty Insolent brute!   515

Lady Fidget Brute! Stinking, mortified, rotten French
wether, to dare –

Sir Jaspar Hold, an't please your ladyship. – For shame,
Master Horner, your mother was a woman. [*Aside*]
Now shall I never reconcile 'em. [*Aside to* LADY   520
FIDGET] Hark you, madam, take my advice in your
anger. You know you often want one to make up your
drolling pack of ombre players; and you may cheat
him easily, for he's an ill gamester and consequently

528 *crazy:* frail, sickly, worn-out

538 *fine:* pay (as in pay a fine or forfeit)

539 *wheedle:* swindle or manipulate. Much of the enjoyment of this scene derives from Sir Jaspar's mistaken sense that he is in ultimate control of events – the biter is being bitten!

545 *gazettes:* journals or magazines

546 *shocks:* poodles. Ladies frequently kept small lapdogs about them when at home.

receipts: recipes

loves play. Besides, you know, you have but two old   525
civil gentlemen, with stinking breaths too, to wait
upon you abroad; take in the third into your service.
The other are but crazy; and a lady should have a
supernumerary gentleman-usher, as a supernumerary
coach-horse, lest sometimes you should be forced to   530
stay at home.

LADY FIDGET But are you sure he loves play and has money?

SIR JASPAR He loves play as much as you and has money as
much as I.

LADY FIDGET Then I am contented to make him pay for his   535
scurrility; money makes up in a measure all other
wants in men. [*Aside*] Those whom we cannot make
hold for gallants, we make fine.

SIR JASPAR [*aside*] So, so; now to mollify, to wheedle him.
– Master Horner, will you never keep civil company?   540
Methinks 'tis time now, since you are only fit for them.
Come, come, man, you must e'en fall to visiting our
wives, eating at our tables, drinking tea with our
virtuous relations after dinner, dealing cards to 'em,
reading plays and gazettes to 'em, picking fleas out of   545
their shocks for 'em, collecting receipts, new songs,
women, pages and footmen for 'em.

HORNER I hope they'll afford me better employment, sir.

SIR JASPAR Heh, he, he! 'Tis fit you know your work
before you come into your place; and since you are   550
unprovided of a lady to flatter and a good house to eat
at, pray frequent mine and call my wife mistress and
she shall call you gallant, according to the custom.

HORNER Who, I?

SIR JASPAR Faith, thou shalt for my sake; come, for my   555
sake only.

HORNER For your sake –

SIR JASPAR [*to* LADY FIDGET] Come, come, here's a
gamester for you; let him be a little familiar sometimes.

562 *have a privilege:* have rights or advantages

578–9 *(aside) I think I know her already, therefore may venture with her, my secret for hers:* a key moment in the plot. Horner reveals that the rumour of impotence is simply a cover story. How do you imagine that Lady Fidget, who has certainly been intimately acquainted with Horner before, would register her reaction verbally and physically (eg facial gestures)? Look, too, at her 'perfectly' speech (ll. 590–598).

580 *cuz:* a corruption of 'cousin'. The word often means no more than a close friend, rather than a relative as in modern English.

Nay, what if a little rude? Gamesters may be rude with   560
ladies, you know.

Lady Fidget Yes, losing gamesters have a privilege with
women.

Horner I always thought the contrary, that the winning
gamester had most privilege with women, for when   565
you have lost your money to a man, you'll lose
anything you have, all you have, they say, and he may
use you as he pleases.

Sir Jaspar Heh, he, he! Well, win or lose, you shall have
your liberty with her.   570

Lady Fidget As he behaves himself; and for your sake I'll
give him admittance and freedom.

Horner All sorts of freedom, madam?

Sir Jaspar Ay, ay, ay, all sorts of freedom thou canst take,
and so go to her, begin thy new employment; wheedle   575
her, jest with her and be better acquainted one with
another.

Horner [*aside*] I think I know her already, therefore may
venture with her, my secret for hers.

　　　[HORNER *and* LADY FIDGET *whisper*.]

Sir Jaspar Sister, cuz, I have provided an innocent   580
playfellow for you there.

Dainty Who, he!

Squeamish There's a playfellow indeed!

Sir Jaspar Yes, sure; what, he is good enough to play at
cards, blindman's buff, or the fool with sometimes.   585

Squeamish Foh, we'll have no such playfellows.

Dainty No, sir, you shan't choose playfellows for us, we
thank you.

Sir Jaspar Nay, pray hear me. [*Whispering to them*]

Lady Fidget [*aside to* HORNER] But, poor gentleman,   590
could you be so generous, so truly a man of honour, as
for the sakes of us women of honour, to cause yourself
to be reported no man? No man! And to suffer

607 *be bound with you:* testifying on your behalf

611–12 *to save you harmless:* to secure you from harm by scandal

618 *obscenely:* openly

620 *recovered:* got rid of

yourself the greatest shame that could fall upon a man,
that none might fall upon us women by your   595
conversation? But indeed, sir, as perfectly, perfectly the
same man as before your going into France, sir? As
perfectly, perfectly, sir?

HORNER As perfectly, perfectly, madam. Nay, I scorn you
should take my word; I desire to be tried only, madam.   600

LADY FIDGET Well, that's spoken again like a man of
honour; all men of honour desire to come to the test.
But, indeed, generally you men report such things of
yourselves, one does not know how or whom to
believe and it is come to that pass we dare not take   605
your words, no more than your tailors, without some
staid servant of yours be bound with you. But I have
so strong a faith in your honour, dear, dear, noble sir,
that I'd forfeit mine for yours at any time, dear sir.

HORNER No, madam, you should not need to forfeit it for   610
me; I have given you security already to save you
harmless, my late reputation being so well known in
the world, madam.

LADY FIDGET But if upon any future falling out or upon a
suspicion of my taking the trust out of your hands to   615
employ some other, you yourself should betray your
trust, dear sir? I mean, if you'll give me leave to speak
obscenely, you might tell, dear sir.

HORNER If I did, nobody would believe me; the reputation
of impotency is as hardly recovered again in the world   620
as that of cowardice, dear madam.

LADY FIDGET Nay then, as one may say, you may do your
worst, dear, dear sir.

SIR JASPAR Come, is your ladyship reconciled to him yet?
Have you agreed on matters? For I must be gone to   625
Whitehall.

LADY FIDGET Why, indeed, Sir Jaspar, Master Horner is a
thousand, thousand times a better man than I thought

645–6 How does Wycherley create a sense of completeness at the end of the scene? Look particularly at the message enclosed in the final couplet. In what sense is this ironic?

him. Cousin Squeamish, Sister Dainty, I can name him
now; truly, not long ago, you know, I thought his very   630
name obscenity and I would as soon have lain with
him as have named him.

SIR JASPAR Very likely, poor madam.

DAINTY I believe it.

SQUEAMISH No doubt on't.   635

SIR JASPAR Well, well – that your ladyship is as virtuous as
any she, I know, and him all the town knows – heh,
he, he! Therefore, now you like him, get you gone to
your business together; go, go to your business, I say,
pleasure, whilst I go to my pleasure, business.   640

LADY FIDGET Come then, dear gallant.

HORNER Come away, my dearest mistress.

SIR JASPAR So, so. Why, 'tis as I'd have it.
    [*Exit* SIR JASPAR.]

HORNER And as I'd have it.

LADY FIDGET Who for his business from his wife will run;   645
    Takes the best care to have her business done.
    [*Exeunt omnes.*]

Act III, Scene I

We now see Pinchwife's response to his discovery that his wife was spotted by the gallants at the theatre – he knows that they will be on the lookout for her now!

---

12 *pure:* fine, enjoyable

13 *junketings:* merrymaking, having fun

15 *ninepins:* a fashionable game in the Restoration period

22 *confessor:* one setting a good moral example

23–5 *a confessor ... taught him to do't:* Unscrupulous ostlers (servants at an inn who had care over the horses) would grease a horse's teeth, which supposedly stopped it eating, but still charge the owner for the uneaten feed. Alithea's point, of course, is that Pinchwife himself is mainly responsible for stimulating Margery's interest in the town pleasures.

Act Three   Scene One

[ALITHEA *and* MRS PINCHWIFE.]

ALITHEA Sister, what ails you? You are grown melancholy.

MRS PINCHWIFE Would it not make anyone melancholy to
see you go every day fluttering about abroad, whilst I
must stay at home like a poor, lonely, sullen bird in a
cage?   5

ALITHEA Ay, sister, but you came young and just from the
nest to your cage, so that I thought you liked it and
could be as cheerful in't as others that took their flight
themselves early and are hopping abroad in the open
air.   10

MRS PINCHWIFE Nay, I confess I was quiet enough till my
husband told me what pure lives the London ladies live
abroad, with their dancing, meetings and junketings,
and dressed every day in their best gowns, and, I
warrant you, play at ninepins every day of the week,   15
so they do.

[*Enter* MR PINCHWIFE.]

PINCHWIFE Come, what's here to do? You are putting the
town pleasures in her head and setting her a-longing.

ALITHEA Yes, after ninepins; you suffer none to give her
those longings, you mean, but yourself.   20

PINCHWIFE I tell her of the vanities of the town like a
confessor.

ALITHEA A confessor! Just such a confessor as he that, by
forbidding a silly ostler to grease the horse's teeth,
taught him to do't.   25

PINCHWIFE Come, Mistress Flippant, good precepts are lost
when bad examples are still before us; the liberty you
take abroad makes her hanker after it, and out of

33 *go abroad:* go out

45–82 Notice how quickly here Margery is becoming 'a town wife'. She has no desire at all to return to the country and is exhibiting the traditional symptoms of town wives when they don't get their own way – moodiness, claiming to be unwell, etc. However, she retains her country naivety by openly telling her husband why she wants to go to a play ('to look upon the playermen'), a reason, no doubt, very common amongst Restoration audiences.

61 *receipt-book:* a sort of medical reference book

humour at home, poor wretch! She desired not to
come to London; I would bring her.   30

Alithea Very well.

Pinchwife She has been this week in town and never
desired, till this afternoon, to go abroad.

Alithea Was she not at a play yesterday?

Pinchwife Yes, but she ne'er asked me; I was myself the   35
cause of her going.

Alithea Then, if she ask you again, you are the cause of
her asking, and not my example.

Pinchwife Well, tomorrow night I shall be rid of you and
the next day, before 'tis light, she and I'll be rid of the   40
town, and my dreadful apprehensions. [*To* MRS
PINCHWIFE] Come, be not melancholy, for thou
shalt go into the country after tomorrow, dearest.

Alithea Great comfort!

Mrs Pinchwife Pish, what d'ye tell me of the country for?   45

Pinchwife How's this! What, pish at the country!

Mrs Pinchwife Let me alone, I am not well.

Pinchwife Oh, if that be all – what ails my dearest?

Mrs Pinchwife Truly I don't know; but I have not been
well since you told me there was a gallant at the play   50
in love with me.

Pinchwife Ha –

Alithea That's by my example too!

Pinchwife Nay, if you are not well, but are so concerned
because a lewd fellow chanced to lie and say he liked   55
you, you'll make me sick too.

Mrs Pinchwife Of what sickness?

Pinchwife O, of that which is worse than the plague,
jealousy.

Mrs Pinchwife Pish, you jeer! I'm sure there's no such   60
disease in our receipt-book at home.

Pinchwife No, thou never met'st with it, poor innocent.
[*Aside*] Well, if thou cuckold me, 'twill be my own

64–5 Pinchwife here is punning on the phrase, 'makers of their own fortune'. Cuckolds are 'makers' in the sense that they themselves are to blame for being cuckolded. Bastards have to make their own way in the world ('make their own fortunes') since, being illegitimate, they will not inherit anything from their fathers. Note how Pinchwife's status as a cuckold does not debar him from making perceptive and witty remarks.

70 *pin:* bit

76 *abroad:* out

82 *once:* once and for all

95 *chariot-wheel:* wheel of a carriage

fault – for cuckolds and bastards are generally makers
of their own fortune.   65

MRS PINCHWIFE Well, but pray, bud, let's go to a play
tonight.

PINCHWIFE 'Tis just done, she comes from it. But why are
you so eager to see a play?

MRS PINCHWIFE Faith, dear, not that I care one pin for their   70
talk there; but I like to look upon the playermen and
would see, if I could, the gallant you say loves me;
that's all, dear bud.

PINCHWIFE Is that all, dear bud?

ALITHEA This proceeds from my example.   75

MRS PINCHWIFE But if the play be done, let's go abroad,
however, dear bud.

PINCHWIFE Come, have a little patience and thou shalt go
into the country on Friday.

MRS PINCHWIFE Therefore I would see first some sights, to   80
tell my neighbours of. Nay, I will go abroad, that's
once.

ALITHEA I'm the cause of this desire too.

PINCHWIFE But now I think on't, who was the cause of
Horner's coming to my lodging today? That was you.   85

ALITHEA No, you, because you would not let him see your
handsome wife out of your lodging.

MRS PINCHWIFE Why, O Lord! Did the gentleman come
hither to see me indeed?

PINCHWIFE No, no. – You are not cause of that damned   90
question too, Mistress Alithea? [*Aside*] Well, she's in
the right of it. He is in love with my wife – and comes
after her – 'tis so – but I'll nip his love in the bud, lest
he should follow us into the country and break his
chariot-wheel near our house on purpose for an excuse   95
to come to't. But I think I know the town.

MRS PINCHWIFE Come, pray, bud, let's go abroad before 'tis
late, for I will go, that's flat and plain.

103 *Let her put on her mask:* The wearing of masks as a fashion accessory had become very popular by 1675. It could either be held in the hand and raised or lowered as desired, or be fixed to the hair with pins. In his *History*, Bishop Burnet recorded in 1688: 'At this time, the court fell into much extravagance in masquerading; both King and Queen and all the court went about masked, and came into houses unknown, and danced there with a great deal of wild frolic.' The practice of masking was complicated by the fact that the prostitutes who frequented the playhouses themselves wore masks as a sign of their trade ('vizard masks') and fine ladies who wished to attend plays incognito had, in effect, to compete with them to attract the attention of the men.

116–21 *So – I have it … 'twould turn his stomach; no, no.':* Pinchwife shows a high degree of awareness here of the dangers of mask-wearing, but, ironically, he fails to realise that dressing Margery up as a young man in close-fitting clothes will actually reveal more of her feminine shape than her own garments. The Restoration audience, familiar with what had become a popular convention of dressing women as men, would know that Pinchwife had certainly made matters worse for himself.

122 *greasy:* filthy, vulgar

PINCHWIFE [*aside*] So! the obstinacy already of a town-wife,
and I must, whilst she's here, humour her like one. –   100
Sister, how shall we do, that she may not be seen or
known?

ALITHEA Let her put on her mask.

PINCHWIFE Pshaw, a mask makes people but the more
inquisitive and is as ridiculous a disguise as a   105
stage-beard; her shape, stature, habit will be known
and if we should meet with Horner, he would be sure
to take acquaintance with us, must wish her joy, kiss
her, talk to her, leer upon her, and the devil and all.
No, I'll not use her to a mask, 'tis dangerous, for   110
masks have made more cuckolds than the best faces
that ever were known.

ALITHEA How will you do then?

MRS PINCHWIFE Nay, shall we go? The Exchange will be
shut, and I have a mind to see that.   115

PINCHWIFE So – I have it – I'll dress her up in the suit we
are to carry down to her brother, little Sir James; nay, I
understand the town tricks. Come, let's go dress her. A
mask! No – a woman masked, like a covered dish,
gives a man curiosity and appetite, when, it may be,   120
uncovered, 'twould turn his stomach; no, no.

ALITHEA Indeed your comparison is something a greasy
one. But I had a gentle gallant used to say, 'A beauty
masked, like the sun in eclipse, gathers together more
gazers than if it shined out.'   125
   [*Exeunt.*]

Act III, Scene II

The scene changes to the New Exchange: see note on Act II, Scene I, lines 3–5 and Resource Notes. Horner attempts to explain to his companions the apparent contradiction in his behaviour: he continues to spend a great deal of time with women, although he claims to desire revenge against them. It is a mark of Horner's single-mindedness that he has not divulged his plan to his best friends.

---

11 *drone:* male bee which produces nothing except noise

15 *beetle-headed:* stupid

liquorish: lecherous

26 *set out your hand:* furnish you with food and drink. Horner's point is that as long as the fool is paying, one can tolerate his company. The remark also links with the following analogies with gambling.

Act Three   Scene Two

[The scene changes to the New Exchange.]

[Enter HORNER, HARCOURT, DORILANT.]

DORILANT Engaged to women, and not sup with us?

HORNER Ay, a pox on 'em all!

HARCOURT You were much a more reasonable man in the
morning and had as noble resolutions against 'em as a
widower of a week's liberty.   5

DORILANT Did I ever think to see you keep company with
women in vain?

HORNER In vain! No – 'tis, since I can't love 'em, to be
revenged on 'em.

HARCOURT Now your sting is gone, you looked in the box   10
amongst all those women, like a drone in the hive, all
upon you, shoved and ill-used by 'em all, and thrust
from one side to t'other.

DORILANT Yet he must be buzzing amongst 'em still, like
other old beetle-headed, liquorish drones. Avoid 'em,   15
and hate 'em as they hate you.

HORNER Because I do hate 'em, and would hate 'em yet
more, I'll frequent 'em; you may see by marriage,
nothing makes a man hate a woman more than her
constant conversation. In short, I converse with 'em, as   20
you do with rich fools, to laugh at 'em and use 'em ill.

DORILANT But I would no more sup with women, unless I
could lie with 'em, than sup with a rich coxcomb,
unless I could cheat him.

HORNER Yes, I have known thee sup with a fool for his   25
drinking; if he could set out your hand that way only,

29–30 *tosses with a marker ... in ure:* plays dice with someone who keeps the scores, not competitively but just for practice

33 *laying 'em flat with a bottle:* getting them drunk

38–9 *decayed fornicators:* those no longer able to perform, or enjoy, sex

41 *civil women:* 'decent' women, ie not wenches. Harcourt is here expressing surprise that Horner should spend time with women who are not necessarily potential sexual partners.

50 *sack and sugar:* Sack is a sweet Spanish white wine, often drunk with sugar at the time, although it would have made the wine very sweet. Harcourt's distaste may also be due to its contemporary connection with invalids.
Compare the attitudes shown by the men here with those in Act I, Scene I. How does it affect your view of the gallants in general? Compare too the way in which Harcourt refers to Alithea in lines 54–55, with the way he actually talks to her later in this scene, and in the play generally.

you were satisfied, and if he were a wine-swallowing
mouth 'twas enough.

HARCOURT Yes, a man drinks often with a fool, as he tosses
with a marker, only to keep his hand in ure. But do the   30
ladies drink?

HORNER Yes, sir, and I shall have the pleasure at least of
laying 'em flat with a bottle, and bring as much
scandal that way upon 'em as formerly t'other.

HARCOURT Perhaps you may prove as weak a brother   35
amongst 'em that way as t'other.

DORILANT Foh, drinking with women is as unnatural as
scolding with 'em; but 'tis a pleasure of decayed
fornicators, and the basest way of quenching love.

HARCOURT Nay, 'tis drowning love instead of quenching it.   40
But leave us for civil women too!

DORILANT Ay, when he can't be the better for 'em. We
hardly pardon a man that leaves his friend for a
wench, and that's a pretty lawful call.

HORNER Faith, I would not leave you for 'em, if they   45
would not drink.

DORILANT Who would disappoint his company at Lewis's
for a gossiping?

HARCOURT Foh, wine and women, good apart, together as
nauseous as sack and sugar. But hark you, sir, before   50
you go, a little of your advice; an old maimed general,
when unfit for action, is fittest for counsel. I have
other designs upon women than eating and drinking
with them. I am in love with Sparkish's mistress, whom
he is to marry tomorrow. Now how shall I get her?   55
    [*Enter* SPARKISH, *looking about.*]

HORNER Why, here comes one will help you to her.

HARCOURT He! He, I tell you, is my rival, and will hinder
my love.

HORNER No, a foolish rival and a jealous husband assist
their rival's designs, for they are sure to make their   60

97

67 *bubbled:* cheated

70 *snack:* share

71 *woodcocks:* gamebirds, or simpletons, those who can be easily tricked

81 *... but I am sure I know myself:* a fairly sure sign, coming from Sparkish, that he doesn't! Lack of self-knowledge is often one of the main character flaws in a fool which makes them ripe for ridicule.

women hate them, which is the first step to their love
for another man.

HARCOURT But I cannot come near his mistress but in his
company.

HORNER Still the better for you, for fools are most easily   65
cheated when they themselves are accessories; and he is
to be bubbled of his mistress, as of his money, the
common mistress, by keeping him company.

SPARKISH Who is that, that is to be bubbled? Faith, let me
snack, I han't met with a bubble since Christmas. Gad,   70
I think bubbles are like their brother woodcocks, go
out with the cold weather.

HARCOURT [*apart to* HORNER] A pox! He did not hear
all, I hope.

SPARKISH Come, you bubbling rogues you, where do we   75
sup? – Oh, Harcourt, my mistress tells me you have
been making fierce love to her all the play long, hah,
ha! But I –

HARCOURT I make love to her?

SPARKISH Nay, I forgive thee, for I think I know thee, and   80
I know her, but I am sure I know myself.

HARCOURT Did she tell you so? I see all women are like
these of the Exchange, who, to enhance the price of
their commodities, report to their fond customers
offers which were never made 'em.   85

HORNER Ay, women are as apt to tell before the intrigue as
men after it, and so show themselves the vainer sex.
But hast thou a mistress, Sparkish? 'Tis as hard for me
to believe it as that thou ever hadst a bubble, as you
bragged just now.   90

SPARKISH Oh, your servant, sir; are you at your raillery,
sir? But we were some of us beforehand with you
today at the play. The wits were something bold with
you, sir; did you not hear us laugh?

95–148 *Yes, but I thought you had gone to plays ... and all readers, courteous or uncourteous:* These lines, which are generally cut from modern productions, constitute the most extensive comment in the play on the relationship between the stage and the audience. Sparkish is presented as a typical 'pit performer' and the gallants' questions effectively provide him with a platform to demonstrate his foolishness and vanity. What seems to you to be Sparkish's main complaint about 'poets' (playwrights)? Do you detect any attempt here by Wycherley to define the function of Restoration drama?

114 *playing with fans:* Like the mask, the fan had by this time become a vital social accoutrement in the lovers' armoury (see page 267 in the Resource Notes).

115 *Phyllis:* used here as an example of a typical female name

121 *burlesque:* a parody or 'send up'

123 *hictius doctius, topsy-turvy:* terms used by stage jugglers

Horner Yes, but I thought you had gone to plays to laugh 95
at the poet's wit, not at your own.

Sparkish Your servant, sir; no, I thank you. Gad, I go to a
play as to a country treat; I carry my own wine to one
and my own wit to t'other, or else I'm sure I should
not be merry at either. And the reason why we are so 100
often louder than the players is because we think we
speak more wit and so become the poet's rivals in his
audience. For to tell you the truth, we hate the silly
rogues, nay, so much that we find fault even with their
bawdy upon the stage, whilst we talk nothing else in 105
the pit as loud.

Horner But why shouldst thou hate the silly poets? Thou
hast too much wit to be one, and they, like whores, are
only hated by each other – and thou dost scorn
writing, I'm sure. 110

Sparkish Yes, I'd have you to know I scorn writing; but
women, women, that make men do all foolish things,
make 'em write songs too. Everybody does it. 'Tis even
as common with lovers as playing with fans; and you
can no more help rhyming to your Phyllis than 115
drinking to your Phyllis.

Harcourt Nay, poetry in love is no more to be avoided
than jealousy.

Dorilant But the poets damned your songs, did they?

Sparkish Damn the poets! They turned 'em into 120
burlesque, as they call it. That burlesque is a
hocus-pocus trick they have got, which, by virtue of
hictius doctius, topsy-turvy, they make a wise and
witty man in the world a fool upon the stage, you
know not how; and 'tis therefore I hate 'em too, for I 125
know not but it may be my own case, for they'll put a
man into a play for looking asquint. Their
predecessors were contented to make serving-men only
their stage-fools, but these rogues must have

139 *as:* equally

143 *like:* realistically

149 Stage direction *(Enter Mr Pinchwife and his wife in man's clothes ...):* This is potentially one of the funniest entrances in the play. How should Pinchwife and Margery conduct themselves about the stage here? There should certainly be no doubt at all, as far as the audience is concerned, that Margery is really female!

150 *Oh, hide me!:* How should this piece of stage business be handled to create comedy?

153 *fail the drawing room:* let down those who await my company. The drawing room was the usual place to receive visitors.

gentlemen, with a pox to 'em, nay, knights; and, 130
indeed, you shall hardly see a fool upon the stage but
he's a knight and, to tell you the truth, they have kept
me these six years from being a knight in earnest, for
fear of being knighted in a play, and dubbed a fool.

DORILANT Blame 'em not; they must follow their copy, the 135
age.

HARCOURT But why shouldst thou be afraid of being in a
play, who expose yourself every day in the playhouses
and as public places?

HORNER 'Tis but being on the stage, instead of standing on 140
a bench in the pit.

DORILANT Don't you give money to painters to draw you
like? And are you afraid of your pictures at length in a
playhouse, where all your mistresses may see you?

SPARKISH A pox! Painters don't draw the smallpox or 145
pimples in one's face. Come, damn all your silly
authors whatever, all books and booksellers, by the
world, and all readers, courteous or uncourteous.

HARCOURT But who comes here, Sparkish?

[*Enter* MR PINCHWIFE *and his wife in man's clothes,*
ALITHEA, LUCY *her maid.*]

SPARKISH Oh, hide me! There's my mistress too. 150

[SPARKISH *hides himself behind* HARCOURT]

HARCOURT She sees you.

SPARKISH But I will not see her. 'Tis time to go to
Whitehall and I must not fail the drawing room.

HARCOURT Pray, first carry me, and reconcile me to her.

SPARKISH Another time; faith, the King will have supped. 155

HARCOURT Not with the worse stomach for thy absence;
thou art one of those fools that think their attendance
at the King's meals as necessary as his physicians',
when you are more troublesome to him than his
doctors, or his dogs. 160

SPARKISH Pshaw, I know my interest, sir. Prithee hide me.

167 *Clasp: We have no ballads:*   Clasp is a street vendor.

168–70 *Then give me … I'll have them:*   The texts which Margery requests are very out of date, thereby making a comment on country tastes. *Covent Garden Drollery* would have contained pieces by Wycherley himself.

177 *Let us follow 'em:*   Pinchwife has failed and the hunt is on!

179 *fain be:*   would like to be

185 *never go:*   'don't worry' or 'be assured'

HORNER Your servant, Pinchwife. – What, he knows us
    not!

PINCHWIFE [*to his wife aside*] Come along.

MRS PINCHWIFE Pray, have you any ballads? Give me   165
    sixpenny worth.

CLASP We have no ballads.

MRS PINCHWIFE Then give me *Covent Garden Drollery*, and
    a play or two – Oh, here's *Tarugo's Wiles*, and *The
    Slighted Maiden*; I'll have them.   170

PINCHWIFE [*apart to her*] No, plays are not for your
    reading. Come along; will you discover yourself?

HORNER Who is that pretty youth with him, Sparkish?

SPARKISH I believe his wife's brother, because he's
    something like her, but I never saw her but once.   175

HORNER Extremely handsome; I have seen a face like it
    too. Let us follow 'em.

    [*Exeunt* PINCHWIFE, MRS PINCHWIFE, ALITHEA,
    LUCY; HORNER, DORILANT *following them.*]

HARCOURT Come, Sparkish, your mistress saw you and will
    be angry you go not to her. Besides, I would fain be
    reconciled to her, which none but you can do, dear   180
    friend.

SPARKISH Well, that's a better reason, dear friend. I would
    not go near her now, for hers or my own sake, but I
    can deny you nothing, for though I have known thee a
    great while, never go, if I do not love thee as well as a   185
    new acquaintance.

HARCOURT I am obliged to you indeed, dear friend. I would
    be well with her, only to be well with thee still, for
    these ties to wives usually dissolve all ties to friends. I
    would be contented she should enjoy you a-nights, but   190
    I would have you to myself a-days, as I have had, dear
    friend.

196–201 *So, we are hard put ... other cloaks:* What impression do you gain of Harcourt from this speech? Do you have any sympathy for Sparkish?

201 Stage direction *(Re-enter Mr Pinchwife, Mrs Pinchwife ...):* This scene would have made extensive use of the two stage doors on each side of the stage when first performed at the Theatre Royal (see pages 274–275 in the Resource Notes). This is referred to explicitly in the next stage direction at line 220.

205 *seamstresses:* assistant dressmakers

209–10 How does Mrs Pinchwife speak these lines to convince others she is a man?

215 *proper sign:* cuckold's horns (like bulls, stags or rams)

SPARKISH And thou shalt enjoy me a-days, dear, dear
     friend, never stir, and I'll be divorced from her sooner
     than from thee. Come along.   195
HARCOURT [aside] So, we are hard put to't when we make
     our rival our procurer; but neither she nor her brother
     would let me come near her now. When all's done, a
     rival is the best cloak to steal to a mistress under,
     without suspicion, and when we have once got to her   200
     as we desire, we throw him off like other cloaks.
          [Exit SPARKISH, and HARCOURT following him.]
          [Re-enter MR PINCHWIFE, MRS PINCHWIFE in man's
          clothes.]
PINCHWIFE [to ALITHEA (off-stage)] Sister, if you will not
     go, we must leave you. [Aside] The fool her gallant
     and she will muster up all the young saunterers of this
     place, and they will leave their dear seamstresses to   205
     follow us. What a swarm of cuckolds and
     cuckold-makers are here! – Come, let's be gone,
     Mistress Margery.
MRS PINCHWIFE Don't you believe that; I han't half my
     bellyful of sights yet.   210
PINCHWIFE Then walk this way.
MRS PINCHWIFE Lord, what a power of brave signs are here!
     Stay – the Bull's-Head, the Ram's-Head and the
     Stag's-Head, dear –
PINCHWIFE Nay, if every husband's proper sign here were   215
     visible, they would be all alike.
MRS PINCHWIFE What d'ye mean by that, bud?
PINCHWIFE 'Tis no matter – no matter, bud.
MRS PINCHWIFE Pray tell me; nay, I will know.
PINCHWIFE They would be all bulls', stags' and rams' heads.   220
          [Exeunt MR PINCHWIFE, MRS PINCHWIFE.]
          [Re-enter SPARKISH, HARCOURT, ALITHEA, LUCY,
          at t'other door.]

221–373 *Come, dear madam … Come, pray, madam, be friends with him:* This is one of the main 'set-pieces' in the play for the Harcourt–Alithea–Sparkish triangle. As you read it, think about how Wycherley conveys Harcourt's wit, Sparkish's foolishness and Alithea's growing bewilderment. What prevents the scene from being 'romantic' in the conventional sense?

249 *argues:* exposes, emphasises

Sparkish Come, dear madam, for my sake you shall be reconciled to him.

Alithea For your sake I hate him.

Harcourt That's something too cruel, madam, to hate me for his sake.   225

Sparkish Ay indeed, madam, too, too cruel to me, to hate my friend for my sake.

Alithea I hate him because he is your enemy; and you ought to hate him too, for making love to me, if you love me.   230

Sparkish That's a good one! I hate a man for loving you! If he did love you, 'tis but what he can't help and 'tis your fault, not his, if he admires you. I hate a man for being of my opinion! I'll ne'er do't by the world.

Alithea Is it for your honour or mine, to suffer a man to   235
make love to me, who am to marry you tomorrow?

Sparkish Is it for your honour or mine, to have me jealous? That he makes love to you is a sign you are handsome and that I am not jealous is a sign you are virtuous. That, I think, is for your honour.   240

Alithea But 'tis your honour too I am concerned for.

Harcourt But why, dearest madam, will you be more concerned for his honour than he is himself? Let his honour alone, for my sake and his. He, he has no honour –   245

Sparkish How's that?

Harcourt But what my dear friend can guard himself.

Sparkish O ho – that's right again.

Harcourt Your care of his honour argues his neglect of it, which is no honour to my dear friend here; therefore   250
once more, let his honour go which way it will, dear madam.

Sparkish Ay, ay, were it for my honour to marry a woman whose virtue I suspected and could not trust her in a friend's hands?   255

262 *jealous:* Not the usual meaning here, but over-excited or over-wrought. Alithea deliberately uses a pun to bring to mind the modern meaning in line 267.

273 *easy:* unconcerned

276 *thrown away upon her:* is wasted on her, ie not good enough for her

277 *None to:* There is no one like. Wycherley here provides a rare view of how the gentry are seen by the 'lower orders'.

ALITHEA Are you not afraid to lose me?

HARCOURT He afraid to lose you, madam! No, no – you may see how the most estimable and most glorious creature in the world is valued by him. Will you not see it? 260

SPARKISH Right, honest Frank, I have that noble value for her that I cannot be jealous of her.

ALITHEA You mistake him, he means you care not for me, nor who has me.

SPARKISH Lord, madam, I see you are jealous. Will you 265 wrest a poor man's meaning from his words?

ALITHEA You astonish me, sir, with your want of jealousy.

SPARKISH And you make me giddy, madam, with your jealousy and fears and virtue and honour. Gad, I see virtue makes a woman as troublesome as a little 270 reading or learning.

ALITHEA Monstrous!

LUCY [behind] Well, to see what easy husbands these women of quality can meet with; a poor chambermaid can never have such lady-like luck. Besides, he's 275 thrown away upon her; she'll make no use of her fortune, her blessing. None to a gentleman for a pure cuckold, for it requires good breeding to be a cuckold.

ALITHEA I tell you then plainly, he pursues me to marry me.

SPARKISH Pshaw! 280

HARCOURT Come, madam, you see you strive in vain to make him jealous of me; my dear friend is the kindest creature in the world to me.

SPARKISH Poor fellow.

HARCOURT But his kindness only is not enough for me, 285 without your favour; your good opinion, dear madam, 'tis that must perfect my happiness. Good gentleman, he believes all I say – would you would do so. Jealous of me! I would not wrong him nor you for the world.

291 Stage direction *(carelessly):* unconcernedly

298 Stage direction *(Clapping his hand on his breast, points at Sparkish):* This sequence of gestures requires considerable control and timing. How would you position the players to maximise the comic effect?

305 *injure:* insult

Sparkish Look you there; hear him, hear him, and do not   290
    walk away so.
    [ALITHEA *walks carelessly to and fro.*]
Harcourt I love you, madam, so –
Sparkish How's that! Nay – now you begin to go too far
    indeed.
Harcourt So much, I confess, I say I love you, that I   295
    would not have you miserable and cast yourself away
    upon so unworthy and inconsiderable a thing as what
    you see here.
    [*Clapping his hand on his breast, points at* SPARKISH]
Sparkish No, faith, I believe thou wouldst not; now his
    meaning is plain. But I knew before thou wouldst not   300
    wrong me nor her.
Harcourt No, no, heavens forbid the glory of her sex
    should fall so low as into the embraces of such a
    contemptible wretch, the last of mankind – my dear
    friend here – I injure him? [*Embracing* SPARKISH]   305
Alithea Very well.
Sparkish No, no, dear friend, I knew it. – Madam, you
    see he will rather wrong himself than me, in giving
    himself such names.
Alithea Do not you understand him yet?   310
Sparkish Yes, how modestly he speaks of himself, poor
    fellow.
Alithea Methinks he speaks impudently of yourself, since
    – before yourself too; insomuch that I can no longer
    suffer his scurrilous abusiveness to you, no more than   315
    his love to me. [*Offers to go*]
Sparkish Nay, nay, madam, pray stay – his love to you!
    Lord, madam, he has not spoke yet plain enough?
Alithea Yes, indeed, I should think so.
Sparkish Well then, by the world, a man can't speak   320
    civilly to a woman now but presently she says he
    makes love to her. Nay, madam, you shall stay, with

324 *éclaircissement:* a full explanation; a typically extravagant and affected Sparkish turn of phrase

326 *catechism:* a question and answer technique designed to test someone's knowledge and, in its original religious context, their devotion. How does the use of this device by Wycherley affect the pace of the scene? Can you detect precisely how it works?

333 *out:* mistaken

349 *Who:* The sense of this word is carried over from line 345. Harcourt is not asking a question – he is referring to himself in the form of a rhetorical question.

your pardon, since you have not yet understood him,
till he has made an éclaircissement of his love to you,
that is, what kind of love it is. [*To* HARCOURT]   325
Answer to thy catechism. Friend, do you love my
mistress here?

HARCOURT Yes, I wish she would not doubt it.

SPARKISH But how do you love her?

HARCOURT With all my soul.   330

ALITHEA I thank him; methinks he speaks plain enough
now.

SPARKISH [*to* ALITHEA] You are out still. – But with what
kind of love, Harcourt?

HARCOURT With the best and truest love in the world.   335

SPARKISH Look you there then, that is with no
matrimonial love, I'm sure.

ALITHEA How's that? Do you say matrimonial love is not
best?

SPARKISH Gad, I went too far ere I was aware. But speak   340
for thyself, Harcourt; you said you would not wrong
me nor her.

HARCOURT No, no, madam, e'en take him for heaven's sake –

SPARKISH Look you there, madam.

HARCOURT Who should in all justice be yours, he that loves   345
you most.

[*Claps his hand on his breast*]

ALITHEA Look you there, Mr Sparkish, who's that?

SPARKISH Who should it be? – Go on, Harcourt.

HARCOURT Who loves you more than women titles or
fortune fools.   350

[*Points at* SPARKISH]

SPARKISH Look you there, he means me still, for he points
at me.

ALITHEA Ridiculous!

HARCOURT Who can only match your faith and constancy
in love.   355

367 *in fine:* to conclude

373–406 Stage direction *(Enter Mr Pinchwife, Mrs Pinchwife ... Good night, dear Harcourt):* Note Pinchwife's role during this section. When dealing with his sister's affairs he is far more perceptive than in dealing with his own. Wycherley uses one fool (Pinchwife) to help expose another (Sparkish).

381 *frank:* candid, open. There is a further rather weak joke here in that Frank is Harcourt's first name. Pinchwife makes considerable use of its further meaning of 'generous' in the succeeding lines. It also has a connotation of 'sexually loose'.

384 *menial:* domestic, part of the household

Sparkish Ay.

Harcourt Who knows, if it be possible, how to value so
much beauty and virtue.

Sparkish Ay.

Harcourt Whose love can no more be equalled in the   360
world than that heavenly form of yours.

Sparkish No.

Harcourt Who could no more suffer a rival than your
absence, and yet could no more suspect your virtue
than his own constancy in his love to you.   365

Sparkish No.

Harcourt Who, in fine, loves you better than his eyes that
first made him love you.

Sparkish Ay – nay, madam, faith, you shan't go till –

Alithea Have a care, lest you make me stay too long –   370

Sparkish But till he has saluted you, that I may be assured
you are friends, after his honest advice and
declaration. Come, pray, madam, be friends with him.
[*Enter* MR PINCHWIFE, MRS PINCHWIFE.]

Alithea You must pardon me, sir, that I am not yet so
obedient to you.   375

Pinchwife What, invite your wife to kiss men? Monstrous!
Are you not ashamed? I will never forgive you.

Sparkish Are you not ashamed that I should have more
confidence in the chastity of your family than you
have? You must not teach me. I am a man of honour,   380
sir, though I am frank and free; I am frank, sir –

Pinchwife Very frank, sir, to share your wife with your
friends.

Sparkish He is an humble, menial friend, such as
reconciles the differences of the marriage bed. You   385
know man and wife do not always agree; I design him
for that use, therefore would have him well with my
wife.

405 *canonical gentleman:* Sparkish's fanciful way of referring to a
vicar or priest who can perform the marriage ceremony

417 *rakehells:* immoral or debauched men

418 Stage direction *(Enter Horner, Dorilant to them):* Here begins
one of the great comic scenes of the play and one of the most
famous in Restoration comedy. When you have read it, identify
what you consider to be its outstanding features and what is
required by a director to maximise its dramatic and comic
potential.

PINCHWIFE A menial friend! – you will get a great many
    menial friends by showing your wife as you do.   390
SPARKISH What then? It may be I have a pleasure in't, as I
    have to show fine clothes at a playhouse the first day
    and count money before poor rogues.
PINCHWIFE He that shows his wife or money will be in
    danger of having them borrowed sometimes.   395
SPARKISH I love to be envied and would not marry a wife
    that I alone could love; loving alone is as dull as eating
    alone. Is it not a frank age? And I am a frank person.
    And to tell you the truth, it may be I love to have rivals
    in a wife; they make her seem to a man still but as a   400
    kept mistress. And so good night, for I must to
    Whitehall. – Madam, I hope you are now reconciled to
    my friend and so I wish you a good night, madam, and
    sleep if you can, for tomorrow you know I must visit
    you early with a canonical gentleman. Good night,   405
    dear Harcourt.

    [*Exit* SPARKISH.]

HARCOURT Madam, I hope you will not refuse my visit
    tomorrow, if it should be earlier, with a canonical
    gentleman, than Mr Sparkish's.
PINCHWIFE [*coming between* ALITHEA *and* HARCOURT]
    This gentlewoman is yet under my care; therefore you   410
    must yet forbear your freedom with her, sir.
HARCOURT Must, sir!
PINCHWIFE Yes, sir, she is my sister.
HARCOURT 'Tis well she is, sir – for I must be her servant,
    sir. – Madam –   415
PINCHWIFE Come away, sister; we had been gone, if it had
    not been for you, and so avoided these lewd rakehells,
    who seem to haunt us.

    [*Enter* HORNER, DORILANT *to them.*]

HORNER How now, Pinchwife?
PINCHWIFE Your servant.   420

427–8 *... but this pretty young gentleman – [Takes hold of Mrs Pinchwife]*:   Does Horner realise at this point that the 'gentleman' is a lady? By line 433, Pinchwife fears he does, but is that conclusive? Consider what difference it would make to how the scene is played. For example, how could the phrase 'pretty young gentleman' be articulated in different ways?

433 *'Sdeath:*   a corruption of 'God's death' – an exclamation of exasperation

434 *sillily:*   adverb derived from 'silly'

446 *out of countenance:*   make him look embarrassed

453 *jeminy:*   a countrified version of 'Gemini' – a mild oath. A modern equivalent would be 'Wow!'

Horner What, I see a little time in the country makes a
   man turn wild and unsociable and only fit to converse
   with his horses, dogs and his herds.

Pinchwife I have business, sir, and must mind it; your
   business is pleasure, therefore you and I must go   425
   different ways.

Horner Well, you may go on, but this pretty young
   gentleman – [*Takes hold of* MRS PINCHWIFE]

Harcourt The lady –

Dorilant And the maid –   430

Horner Shall stay with us, for I suppose their business is
   the same with ours, pleasure.

Pinchwife [*aside*] 'Sdeath, he knows her, she carries it so
   sillily! Yet if he does not, I should be more silly to
   discover it first.   435

Alithea Pray, let us go, sir.

Pinchwife Come, come –

Horner [*to* MRS PINCHWIFE] Had you not rather stay
   with us? – Prithee, Pinchwife, who is this pretty young
   gentleman?   440

Pinchwife One to whom I'm a guardian. [*Aside*] I wish I
   could keep her out of your hands.

Horner Who is he? I never saw anything so pretty in all
   my life.

Pinchwife Pshaw, do not look upon him so much. He's a   445
   poor bashful youth, you'll put him out of countenance.
   – Come away, brother. [*Offers to take her away*]

Horner Oh, your brother!

Pinchwife Yes, my wife's brother. – Come, come, she'll
   stay supper for us.   450

Horner I thought so, for he is very like her I saw you at
   the play with, whom I told you I was in love with.

Mrs Pinchwife [*aside*] O jeminy! Is this he that was in love
   with me? I am glad on't, I vow, for he's a curious fine

465 *dowdy:* a plain, dull woman

475 *So, So:* What do you think is going through Pinchwife's mind at this moment?

476–8 Between them here, Harcourt and Horner wittily deflate idealised representations of women. Horner's remark especially indicates that his interest in Margery is essentially physical!

484 *I am upon a rack!:* A rack was a medieval instrument of torture, and, in this case, ironically one of Pinchwife's own making. How should the line be delivered to convey his feelings and to create comedy for the audience?

gentleman, and I love him already too. [*To* MR   455
PINCHWIFE] Is this he, bud?

PINCHWIFE [*to his wife*] Come away, come away.

HORNER Why, what haste are you in? Why won't you let
me talk with him?

PINCHWIFE Because you'll debauch him; he's yet young and   460
innocent and I would not have him debauched for
anything in the world. [*Aside*] How she gazes on him!
The devil!

HORNER Harcourt, Dorilant, look you here; this is the
likeness of that dowdy he told us of, his wife. Did you   465
ever see a lovelier creature? The rogue has reason to be
jealous of his wife since she is like him, for she would
make all that see her in love with her.

HARCOURT And as I remember now, she is as like him here
as can be.   470

DORILANT She is indeed very pretty, if she be like him.

HORNER Very pretty? A very pretty commendation! She is
a glorious creature, beautiful beyond all things I ever
beheld.

PINCHWIFE So, So.   475

HARCOURT More beautiful than a poet's first mistress of
imagination.

HORNER Or another man's last mistress of flesh and blood.

MRS PINCHWIFE Nay, now you jeer, sir; pray don't jeer me.

PINCHWIFE Come, come. [*Aside*] By heavens, she'll discover 480
herself!

HORNER I speak of your sister, sir.

PINCHWIFE Ay, but saying she was handsome, if like him,
made him blush. [*Aside*] I am upon a rack!

HORNER Methinks he is so handsome he should not be a   485
man.

PINCHWIFE [*aside*] Oh, there 'tis out! He has discovered
her! I am not able to suffer any longer. [*To his wife*]
Come, come away, I say.

491–2 *... let us torment this jealous rogue a little:* A key element of the scene is how the 'torment' is controlled and all under a surface veneer of civility.

507 *discover herself:* give away her real identity

520 *What do you kiss me for? I am no woman:* a guaranteed laugh from the audience here. How should Margery deliver the line?

HORNER Nay, by your leave, sir, he shall not go yet. – [*To*   490
them] Harcourt, Dorilant, let us torment this jealous
rogue a little.

HARCOURT
           How?
DORILANT

HORNER I'll show you.

PINCHWIFE Come, pray, let him go, I cannot stay fooling   495
any longer. I tell you his sister stays supper for us.

HORNER Does she? Come then, we'll all go sup with her
and thee.

PINCHWIFE No, now I think on't, having stayed so long for
us, I warrant she's gone to bed. [*Aside*] I wish she and   500
I were well out of their hands. – Come, I must rise
early tomorrow, come.

HORNER Well, then, if she be gone to bed, I wish her and
you a good night. But pray, young gentleman, present
my humble service to her.   505

MRS PINCHWIFE Thank you heartily, sir.

PINCHWIFE [*aside*] 'Sdeath! she will discover herself yet in
spite of me. – He is something more civil to you, for
your kindness to his sister, than I am, it seems.

HORNER Tell her, dear sweet little gentleman, for all your   510
brother there, that you have revived the love I had for
her at first sight in the playhouse.

MRS PINCHWIFE But did you love her indeed, and indeed?

PINCHWIFE [*aside*] So, so. – Away, I say.

HORNER Nay, stay. Yes, indeed, and indeed, pray do you   515
tell her so, and give her this kiss from me. [*Kisses her*]

PINCHWIFE [*aside*] O heavens! What do I suffer! Now 'tis
too plain he knows her, and yet –

HORNER And this, and this – [*Kisses her again*]

MRS PINCHWIFE What do you kiss me for? I am no woman.   520

PINCHWIFE [*aside*] So – there, 'tis out. – Come, I cannot,
nor will stay any longer.

527–8 *Ten thousand ulcers ... lips:* Do you find this line amusing, grotesque, or both? What does it reveal about the presentation of Pinchwife's character?

532 *gall:* anger

533–47 Notice the number of rapid and highly contrived entrances and exits here. How do they affect the pace and comedy of the scene?

538 *the next walk:* the adjoining path
Stage direction *(haling away):* physically leading away

541 *present:* give a present to

HORNER Nay, they shall send your lady a kiss too. Here, Harcourt, Dorilant, will you not?

　　[*They kiss her.*]

PINCHWIFE [*aside*] How! Do I suffer this? Was I not　　525
accusing another just now for this rascally patience, in permitting his wife to be kissed before his face? Ten thousand ulcers gnaw away their lips! – Come, come.

HORNER Good night, dear little gentleman. Madam, good night. Farewell, Pinchwife. [*Apart to* HARCOURT　　530
and DORILANT] Did not I tell you I would raise his jealous gall?

　　[*Exeunt* HORNER, HARCOURT *and* DORILANT.]

PINCHWIFE So, they are gone at last; stay, let me see first if the coach be at this door.

　　[*Exit.*]

　　[HORNER, HARCOURT, DORILANT *return.*]

HORNER What, not gone yet? Will you be sure to do as I　　535
desired you, sweet sir?

MRS PINCHWIFE Sweet sir, but what will you give me then?

HORNER Anything. Come away into the next walk.

　　[*Exit* HORNER, *haling away* MRS PINCHWIFE.]

ALITHEA Hold, hold! What d'ye do?

LUCY Stay, stay, hold –　　540

HARCOURT Hold, madam, hold! Let him present him, he'll come presently. Nay, I will never let you go till you answer my question.

LUCY For God's sake, sir, I must follow 'em.

DORILANT No, I have something to present you with too;　　545
you shan't follow them.

　　[ALITHEA, LUCY *struggling with* HARCOURT *and* DORILANT.]

　　[PINCHWIFE *returns.*]

PINCHWIFE Where? – how? – what's become of? – gone! – whither?

127

549–50 What contribution is made to this scene by Lucy and Dorilant? Look, too, at Lucy's lines 580–82

551 *with a pox!:* a curse ('pox' is short for 'smallpox')

555–72 The relatively serious 'romantic' dialogue between Alithea and Harcourt here provides a dramatic contrast with the frenzied words and actions of Pinchwife as he desperately seeks his wife.

575 *the rather:* instead

Lucy He's only gone with the gentleman, who will give
him something, an't please your worship. 550

Pinchwife Something – give him something, with a pox! –
where are they?

Alithea In the next walk only, brother.

Pinchwife Only, only! Where, where?
[*Exit* PINCHWIFE *and returns presently, then goes out
again.*]

Harcourt What's the matter with him? Why so much 555
concerned? But dearest madam –

Alithea Pray let me go, sir; I have said and suffered
enough already.

Harcourt Then you will not look upon nor pity my
sufferings? 560

Alithea To look upon 'em, when I cannot help 'em, were
cruelty, not pity; therefore I will never see you more.

Harcourt Let me then, madam, have my privilege of a
banished lover, complaining or railing, and giving you
but a farewell reason why, if you cannot condescend to 565
marry me, you should not take that wretch, my rival.

Alithea He only, not you, since my honour is engaged so
far to him, can give me a reason why I should not
marry him; but if he be true and what I think him to
me, I must be so to him. Your servant, sir. 570

Harcourt Have women only constancy when 'tis a vice
and, like fortune, only true to fools?

Dorilant [*to* LUCY, *who struggles to get from him*] Thou
shalt not stir, thou robust creature; you see I can deal
with you, therefore you should stay the rather, and be 575
kind.
[*Enter* PINCHWIFE.]

Pinchwife Gone, gone, not to be found! Quite gone! Ten
thousand plagues go with 'em! Which way went they?

Alithea But into t'other walk, brother.

590 Stage direction *(Enter Mrs Pinchwife ... and dried fruit):*
Oranges were associated with sex by virtue of the prostitutes
who plied their trade under the thin disguise of orange-
wenches in the playhouses.

597 *coloured:* red in the face

598 *hold yet:* control myself

602 *city patience:* the patience of a city husband cuckolded by a
gallant

604 Stage direction *(Enter Sir Jaspar Fidget):* Sir Jaspar's entrance
and subsequent comment that 'the ladies stay for you' reminds
us of the main design in Horner's plan and that his brief
excursion with Margery was only a diversion.

Lucy Their business will be done presently sure, an't   580
   please your worship; it can't be long in doing, I'm sure
   on't.

Alithea Are they not there?

Pinchwife No; you know where they are, you infamous
   wretch, eternal shame of your family, which you do   585
   not dishonour enough yourself, you think, but you
   must help her to do it too, thou legion of bawds!

Alithea Good brother –

Pinchwife Damned, damned sister!

Alithea Look you here, she's coming.   590
   [*Enter* MRS PINCHWIFE *in man's clothes, running, with
   her hat under her arm, full of oranges and dried fruit;*
   HORNER *following.*]

Mrs Pinchwife O dear bud, look you here what I have got,
   see!

Pinchwife [*aside, rubbing his forehead*] And what I have
   got here too, which you can't see.

Mrs Pinchwife The fine gentleman has given me better   595
   things yet.

Pinchwife Has he so? [*Aside*] Out of breath and coloured!
   I must hold yet.

Horner I have only given your little brother an orange, sir.

Pinchwife [*to* HORNER] Thank you, sir. [*Aside*] You   600
   have only squeezed my orange, I suppose, and given it
   me again; yet I must have a city patience. [*To his wife*]
   Come, come away.

Mrs Pinchwife Stay, till I have put up my fine things, bud.
   [*Enter* SIR JASPAR FIDGET.]

Sir Jaspar O Master Horner, come, come, the ladies stay   605
   for you; your mistress, my wife, wonders you make
   not more haste to her.

Horner I have stayed this half hour for you here and 'tis
   your fault I am not now with your wife.

627–32 *I rather wish ... the better for't:* irony again as Horner's privilege is referred to. Horner's fun has barely begun.

631 *coming to an estate:* inheriting property

632 *threescore:* sixty

636 *strapper:* 'strapping woman', a rather crude form of address

640 *Good night, sir, forever:* At this point, the audience are left with a host of questions about the outcome of the play: will Harcourt give up his quest now? What other tactics might he have up his sleeve? What is your view of Alithea's conduct and moral standpoint throughout Harcourt's attempts to woo her?

SIR JASPAR But pray, don't let her know so much; the truth   610
on't is, I was advancing a certain project to his Majesty
about – I'll tell you.

HORNER No, let's go and hear it at your house. – Good
night, sweet little gentleman. One kiss more, you'll
remember me now, I hope. [*Kisses her*]   615

DORILANT What, Sir Jaspar, will you separate friends? He
promised to sup with us; and if you take him to your
house, you'll be in danger of our company too.

SIR JASPAR Alas, gentlemen, my house is not fit for you;
there are none but civil women there, which are not fit   620
for your turn. He, you know, can bear with the society
of civil women now, ha, ha, ha! Besides, he's one of
my family – he's – heh, heh, heh!

DORILANT What is he?

SIR JASPAR Faith, my eunuch, since you'll have it, heh, he,   625
he!

[*Exeunt* SIR JASPAR FIDGET, *and* HORNER.]

DORILANT I rather wish thou wert his, or my cuckold.
Harcourt, what a good cuckold is lost there for want
of a man to make him one! Thee and I cannot have
Horner's privilege, who can make use of it.   630

HARCOURT Ay, to poor Horner 'tis like coming to an estate
at threescore, when a man can't be the better for't.

PINCHWIFE Come.

MRS PINCHWIFE Presently, bud.

DORILANT Come, let us go too. [*To* ALITHEA] Madam,   635
your servant. [*To* LUCY] Good night, strapper.

HARCOURT Madam, though you will not let me have a good
day or night, I wish you one; but dare not name the
other half of my wish.

ALITHEA Good night, sir, forever.   640

MRS PINCHWIFE I don't know where to put this here, dear
bud; you shall eat it; nay, you shall have part of the

133

645 What will Pinchwife now do to keep his wife from the gallants? How will Margery behave now that she has tasted 'the pleasures of the town'? Traditionally, the interval is taken at the end of Act III.

fine gentleman's good things, or treat as you call it,
when we come home.

PINCHWIFE Indeed, I deserve it, since I furnished the best   645
part of it.

[*Strikes away the orange*]

The gallant treats, presents, and gives the ball
But 'tis the absent cuckold pays for all.

[*Exeunt.*]

Act IV, Scene I

As you read through this scene, consider how Wycherley uses Lucy's character.

1–6 Lucy begins Act IV with a striking and rather unpleasant simile: the 'streetwise' servant is another common figure in Restoration Comedy. Notice how some of her speeches are similar in content, style and tone to those of the male wits, for example in lines 24–28. What does this suggest to you about Wycherley's conception of the nature of 'wit'?

3 *essence and pulvilio:* scent and perfumed powder

22 *make a conscience of it:* make me feel guilty

25 *wencher:* man who has many lovers

Act Four   Scene One

[*In* PINCHWIFE's *house in the morning.*]

[LUCY, ALITHEA *dressed in new clothes.*]

Lucy Well – madam, now have I dressed you and set you
out with so many ornaments and spent upon you
ounces of essence and pulvilio; and all this for no other
purpose but as people adorn and perfume a corpse for
a stinking secondhand grave – such or as bad I think as   5
Master Sparkish's bed.

Alithea Hold your peace.

Lucy Nay, madam, I will ask you the reason why you
would banish poor Master Harcourt forever from your
sight. How could you be so hardhearted?   10

Alithea 'Twas because I was not hardhearted.

Lucy No, no, 'twas stark love and kindness, I warrant.

Alithea It was so; I would see him no more because I love
him.

Lucy Hey-day, a very pretty reason!   15

Alithea You do not understand me.

Lucy I wish you may yourself.

Alithea I was engaged to marry, you see, another man,
whom my justice will not suffer me to deceive or injure.

Lucy Can there be a greater cheat or wrong done to a   20
man than to give him your person without your heart?
I should make a conscience of it.

Alithea I'll retrieve it for him after I am married a while.

Lucy The woman that marries to love better will be as
much mistaken as the wencher that marries to live   25
better. No, madam, marrying to increase love is like

137

29 *rhetoric:* persuasive words

34 *megrim, or falling sickness:* migraine or epilepsy

44 *stick pin:* refers to one of a maid's main tasks – to help pin up her mistress's hair

45 *natural to:* idiot, compared with

49 *to:* as

57–61 *I am satisfied ... the loss of her honour, her quiet and her –:* It is important to note how Alithea's only reason for remaining betrothed to Sparkish is that he is not jealous.

gaming to become rich; alas, you only lose what little
stock you had before.

Alithea I find by your rhetoric you have been bribed to
betray me.   30

Lucy Only by his merit, that has bribed your heart, you
see, against your word and rigid honour. But what a
devil is this honour! 'Tis sure a disease in the head, like
the megrim, or falling sickness, that always hurries
people away to do themselves mischief. Men lose their   35
lives by it; women what's dearer to 'em, their love, the
life of life.

Alithea Come, pray talk you no more of honour, nor
Master Harcourt. I wish the other would come to
secure my fidelity to him and his right in me.   40

Lucy You will marry him then?

Alithea Certainly. I have given him already my word and
will my hand too, to make it good when he comes.

Lucy Well, I wish I may never stick pin more if he be not
an arrant natural to t'other fine gentleman.   45

Alithea I own he wants the wit of Harcourt, which I will
dispense withal for another want he has, which is want
of jealousy, which men of wit seldom want.

Lucy Lord, madam, what should you do with a fool to
your husband? You intend to be honest, don't you?   50
Then that husbandly virtue, credulity, is thrown away
upon you.

Alithea He only that could suspect my virtue should have
cause to do it; 'tis Sparkish's confidence in my truth
that obliges me to be so faithful to him.   55

Lucy You are not sure his opinion may last.

Alithea I am satisfied 'tis impossible for him to be jealous
after the proofs I have had of him. Jealousy in a
husband – Heaven defend me from it! It begets a
thousand plagues to a poor woman, the loss of her   60
honour, her quiet and her –

67–8 *... she is sent into the country ... to a wife, I think.:* the ultimate fate for a London woman! The original Restoration audience would probably have enjoyed this line a great deal. Lucy develops the point further in lines 69–79.

78–9 *Lincoln's Inn ... Pall Mall:* All are examples of fashionable areas in which to live during the Restoration period.

79 Stage direction *(Enter to them Sparkish and Harcourt dressed like a parson):* How convincing do you feel that Harcourt's disguise should be here?

LUCY And her pleasure.

ALITHEA What d'ye mean, impertinent?

LUCY Liberty is a great pleasure, madam.

ALITHEA I say, loss of her honour, her quiet, nay, her life   65
sometimes, and what's as bad almost, the loss of this
town; that is, she is sent into the country, which is the
last ill usage of a husband to a wife, I think.

LUCY [*aside*] Oh, does the wind lie there? – Then, of
necessity, madam, you think a man must carry his wife   70
into the country, if he be wise. The country is as
terrible, I find, to our young English ladies as a
monastery to those abroad, and, on my virginity, I
think they would rather marry a London gaoler than a
high sheriff of a county, since neither can stir from his   75
employment. Formerly women of wit married fools for
a great estate, a fine seat, or the like, but now 'tis for a
pretty seat only in Lincoln's Inn Fields, St James's
Fields or the Pall Mall.

  [*Enter to them* SPARKISH *and* HARCOURT *dressed like
  a parson.*]

SPARKISH Madam, your humble servant, a happy day to   80
you, and to us all.

HARCOURT Amen.

ALITHEA Who have we here?

SPARKISH My chaplain, faith. O madam, poor Harcourt
remembers his humble service to you and, in obedience   85
to your last commands, refrains coming into your sight.

ALITHEA Is not that he?

SPARKISH No, fie, no; but to show that he ne'er intended
to hinder our match, has sent his brother here to join
our hands. When I get me a wife, I must get her a   90
chaplain, according to the custom; this is his brother,
and my chaplain.

ALITHEA His brother?

94–5 *And your chaplain, to preach in your pulpit then.:* a rather crude innuendo here from Lucy

103 *canonical:* Legal marriages could only be conducted in the Anglican church between 8 am and noon.

110 *sneaking:* sneaky, untrustworthy

121 *in orders:* a minister of the church

Lucy [*aside*] And your chaplain, to preach in your pulpit then. 95

Alithea His brother!

Sparkish Nay, I knew you would not believe it. – I told you, sir, she would take you for your brother Frank.

Alithea Believe it!

Lucy [*aside*] His brother! hah, ha, he! He has a trick left 100
still, it seems.

Sparkish Come, my dearest, pray let us go to church before the canonical hour is past.

Alithea For shame, you are abused still.

Sparkish By the world, 'tis strange now you are so 105
incredulous.

Alithea 'Tis strange you are so credulous.

Sparkish Dearest of my life, hear me. I tell you this is Ned Harcourt of Cambridge; by the world, you see he has a sneaking college look. 'Tis true he's something like his 110
brother Frank and they differ from each other no more than in their age, for they were twins.

Lucy Hah, ha, he!

Alithea Your servant, sir; I cannot be so deceived, though you are. But come, let's hear; how do you know what 115
you affirm so confidently?

Sparkish Why, I'll tell you all. Frank Harcourt coming to me this morning, to wish me joy and present his service to you, I asked him if he could help me to a parson, whereupon he told me he had a brother in 120
town who was in orders and he went straight away and sent him you see there to me.

Alithea Yes, Frank goes and puts on a black coat, then tells you he is Ned; that's all you have for't.

Sparkish Pshaw, pshaw, I tell you by the same token, the 125
midwife put her garter about Frank's neck to know 'em asunder, they were so like.

Alithea Frank tells you this too.

143

132–5 *Lord, if you won't believe one … they are so used to 'em:*
Jokes about the promiscuity of clergymen, especially with
chambermaids, are very common in Restoration plays and
writings, for example from John Phillips' 1655 work *Satyr
Against Hypocrites:*
'There sits a chambermaid upon a hassock
Whom the chaplain oft instructs without his cassock'.
It is rather like the modern joke about 'the actress and the
bishop'. Towards the end of the Restoration, the stage came in
for some fairly severe criticism about its attitude to, and
presentation of, the Church.

148–9 *I had forgot … or I wear it in vain:*   What tone of voice should
Harcourt adopt when impersonating the clergyman?

160–67 *I desire nothing more than to marry you presently …:*   a fairly
well-known pun.

Sparkish Ay, and Ned there too; nay, they are both in a story. 130

Alithea So, so; very foolish!

Sparkish Lord, if you won't believe one, you had best try him by your chambermaid there, for chambermaids must needs know chaplains from other men, they are so used to 'em. 135

Lucy Let's see; nay, I'll be sworn he has the canonical smirk and the filthy, clammy palm of a chaplain.

Alithea Well, most reverend doctor, pray let us make an end of this fooling.

Harcourt With all my soul, divine, heavenly creature, 140 when you please.

Alithea He speaks like a chaplain indeed.

Sparkish Why, was there not 'soul', 'divine', 'heavenly', in what he said?

Alithea Once more, most impertinent black coat, cease 145 your persecution and let us have a conclusion of this ridiculous love.

Harcourt [aside] I had forgot. I must suit my style to my coat, or I wear it in vain.

Alithea I have no more patience left; let us make once an 150 end of this troublesome love, I say.

Harcourt So be it, seraphic lady, when your honour shall think it meet and convenient so to do.

Sparkish Gad, I'm sure none but a chaplain could speak so, I think. 155

Alithea Let me tell you, sir, this dull trick will not serve your turn; though you delay our marriage, you shall not hinder it.

Harcourt Far be it from me, munificent patroness, to delay your marriage. I desire nothing more than to 160 marry you presently, which I might do, if you yourself would, for my noble, good-natured and thrice generous patron here would not hinder it.

166–7 *… I'll die first, for I'm sure I should die after it:* In the second use of the word 'die', Harcourt intends a sexual pun. 'Die' had for long been a rather elaborate metaphor for orgasm.

185 *revokes a hasty doom:* prevents long-term disaster

191–2 *Lord, here's such a deal of modesty:* Sparkish interprets Alithea's reluctance as 'modesty' or shyness. He remains completely ignorant of the truth.

SPARKISH No, poor man, not I, faith.

HARCOURT And now, madam, let me tell you plainly, 165
nobody else shall marry you; by heavens, I'll die first,
for I'm sure I should die after it.

LUCY [aside] How his love has made him forget his
function, as I have seen it in real parsons!

ALITHEA That was spoken like a chaplain too! Now you 170
understand him, I hope.

SPARKISH Poor man, he takes it heinously to be refused. I
can't blame him; 'tis putting an indignity upon him not
to be suffered. But you'll pardon me, madam, it shan't
be, he shall marry us. Come away, pray, madam. 175

LUCY [aside] Hah, ha, he! More ado! 'Tis late.

ALITHEA Invincible stupidity! I tell you he would marry me
as your rival, not as your chaplain.

SPARKISH [pulling her away] Come, come, madam.

LUCY Ay, pray, madam, do not refuse this reverend divine 180
the honour and satisfaction of marrying you, for I dare
say he has set his heart upon't, good doctor.

ALITHEA What can you hope or design by this?

HARCOURT [aside] I could answer her, a reprieve for a day
only often revokes a hasty doom; at worst, if she will 185
not take mercy on me and let me marry her, I have at
least the lover's second pleasure, hindering my rival's
enjoyment, though but for a time.

SPARKISH Come, madam, 'tis e'en twelve o'clock, and my
mother charged me never to be married out of the 190
canonical hours. Come, come. Lord, here's such a deal
of modesty, I warrant, the first day.

LUCY Yes, an't please your worship, married women show
all their modesty the first day, because married men
show all their love the first day. 195

    [Exeunt SPARKISH, ALITHEA, HARCOURT and
    LUCY.]

147

Act IV, Scene II

Pinchwife is subjecting Margery to repeated interrogations about what took place at the New Exchange (Act III, Scene II). Margery's comment in lines 7–8, 'Lord, what pleasure you take to hear it, sure!' is interesting. What is she implying here and how might an actor playing Pinchwife use it to develop his characterisation at this point?

---

15 *China oranges:* the sweetest and most highly prized variety of mandarin oranges

21 *He kissed me an hundred times …:* How does Margery's naivety ('simplicity' – line 33) and honesty contribute to the comedy of this scene as a whole? Alternatively, is she knowingly teasing her husband? (See note on line 71.)

Act Four   Scene Two

[*The scene changes to a bedchamber, where appear*
PINCHWIFE, MRS PINCHWIFE.]

PINCHWIFE Come, tell me, I say.

MRS PINCHWIFE Lord, han't I told it an hundred times over?

PINCHWIFE [*aside*] I would try if, in the repetition of the
ungrateful tale, I could find her altering it in the least
circumstance, for if her story be false, she is so too. –   5
Come, how was't, baggage?

MRS PINCHWIFE Lord, what pleasure you take to hear it,
sure!

PINCHWIFE No, you take more in telling it, I find; but
speak, how was't?   10

MRS PINCHWIFE He carried me up into the house next to the
Exchange.

PINCHWIFE So, and you two were only in the roc n.

MRS PINCHWIFE Yes, for he sent away a youth that was
there, for some dried fruit and China oranges.   15

PINCHWIFE Did he so? Damn him for it – and for –

MRS PINCHWIFE But presently came up the gentlewoman of
the house.

PINCHWIFE O, 'twas well she did; but what did he do whilst
the fruit came?   20

MRS PINCHWIFE He kissed me an hundred times and told me
he fancied he kissed my fine sister, meaning me, you
know, whom he said he loved with all his soul and bid
me be sure to tell her so and to desire her to be at her
window by eleven of the clock this morning and he   25
would walk under it at that time.

PINCHWIFE [*aside*] And he was as good as his word, very
punctual – a pox reward him for't.

42 *mousled:*   pulled about, manhandled

43 *canker:*   ulcerous sore; one of Pinchwife's typically exaggerated curses

50 *changeling:*   fool, idiot

55 Is this speech an aside?

63 *little monster:*   love personified as Cupid

MRS PINCHWIFE Well, and he said if you were not within, he
would come up to her, meaning me, you know, bud,   30
still.

PINCHWIFE [*aside*] So – he knew her certainly; but for this
confession, I am obliged to her simplicity. – But what,
you stood very still when he kissed you?

MRS PINCHWIFE Yes, I warrant you; would you have had me   35
discovered myself?

PINCHWIFE But you told me he did some beastliness to you,
as you called it; what was't?

MRS PINCHWIFE Why, he put –

PINCHWIFE What?   40

MRS PINCHWIFE Why, he put the tip of his tongue between
my lips and so mousled me – and I said, I'd bite it.

PINCHWIFE An eternal canker seize it, for a dog!

MRS PINCHWIFE Nay, you need not be so angry with him
neither, for to say truth, he has the sweetest breath I   45
ever knew.

PINCHWIFE The devil! – you were satisfied with it then, and
would do it again.

MRS PINCHWIFE Not unless he should force me.

PINCHWIFE Force you, changeling! I tell you no woman can   50
be forced.

MRS PINCHWIFE Yes, but she may, sure, by such a one as he,
for he's a proper, goodly strong man; 'tis hard, let me
tell you, to resist him.

PINCHWIFE So, 'tis plain she loves him, yet she has not love 55
enough to make her conceal it from me; but the sight
of him will increase her aversion for me and love for
him and that love instruct her how to deceive me and
satisfy him, all idiot as she is. Love! 'Twas he gave
women first their craft, their art of deluding; out of   60
nature's hands they came plain, open, silly and fit for
slaves, as she and Heaven intended 'em; but damned
love – well – I must strangle that little monster whilst I

68 *invention:* imagination, in the sense of being adept at deception

71 *Come, minx, sit down and write:* Another of the great comic scenes of the play begins here. This extract from a review of one of the first modern revivals of the play in 1924, is illuminating:
'Miss Isabel Jeans played the part with a sort of innocent and affectionate naughtiness that was very attractive. She was not as innocent as she pretended to be, one knew, but she was innocent. Or rather she was only ignorant and the quickest scholar imaginable. It was her ignorance that made her let the cat out of the bag so continually, but when put to it she showed the sharpness of her wits, and her childish delight in them, with the utmost effect. Her first letter scene ... was a perfect piece of acting. The way she showed protest, submission to force, bewilderment, then a dawning sense of a way out, and finally childish triumph, was a lesson in the portrayal of unsophisticated emotions. She was young, lovely and as full of tricks as a monkey.' (Ralph Wright, *New Statesman*, February 1924)

can deal with him. – Go fetch pen, ink and paper out
of the next room.   65
MRS PINCHWIFE Yes, bud.
        [*Exit* MRS PINCHWIFE.]
PINCHWIFE [*aside*] Why should women have more
    invention in love than men? It can only be because
    they have more desires, more soliciting passions, more
    lust, and more of the devil.   70
        [MRS PINCHWIFE *returns.*]
    Come, minx, sit down and write.
MRS PINCHWIFE Ay, dear bud, but I can't do't very well.
PINCHWIFE I wish you could not at all.
MRS PINCHWIFE But what should I write for?
PINCHWIFE I'll have you write a letter to your lover.   75
MRS PINCHWIFE O Lord, to the fine gentleman a letter!
PINCHWIFE Yes, to the fine gentleman.
MRS PINCHWIFE Lord, you do but jeer; sure, you jest.
PINCHWIFE I am not so merry. Come, write as I bid you.
MRS PINCHWIFE What, do you think I am a fool?   80
PINCHWIFE [*aside*] She's afraid I would not dictate any love
    to him, therefore she's unwilling. – But you had best
    begin.
MRS PINCHWIFE Indeed, and indeed, but I won't, so I won't.
PINCHWIFE Why?   85
MRS PINCHWIFE Because he's in town; you may send for him
    if you will.
PINCHWIFE Very well, you would have him brought to you;
    is it come to this? I say, take the pen and write, or
    you'll provoke me.   90
MRS PINCHWIFE Lord, what d'ye make a fool of me for?
    Don't I know that letters are never writ but from the
    country to London and from London into the country?
    Now he's in town and I am in town too; therefore I
    can't write to him, you know.   95

102 *bare 'Sir':* In her innocence, Margery probably provokes her husband further with the prospect of a bare 'Sir'.

104 What might the penknife look like? How should Pinchwife brandish it? Is he genuinely violent?

109 *sweet breath:* This seems to modern readers and audiences an odd way to compliment a lover, but dental hygiene in the seventeenth century was quite basic and most people would have suffered from halitosis ('bad breath') to some degree.

111 A key element in the comedy of this scene is Margery's innocent attempts to compromise with her husband on the choice of language. This, of course, serves only to enrage him still more!

PINCHWIFE [*aside*] So, I am glad it is no worse; she is
    innocent enough yet. – Yes, you may, when your
    husband bids you, write letters to people that are in town.

MRS PINCHWIFE O, may I so? Then I'm satisfied.

PINCHWIFE Come, begin. – [*Dictates*] 'Sir' –   100

MRS PINCHWIFE Shan't I say, 'Dear Sir'? You know one says
    always something more than bare 'Sir'.

PINCHWIFE Write as I bid you, or I will write 'whore' with
    this penknife in your face.

MRS PINCHWIFE Nay, good bud – [*She writes*] 'Sir' –   105

PINCHWIFE 'Though I suffered last night your nauseous,
    loathed kisses and embraces' – Write.

MRS PINCHWIFE Nay, why should I say so? You know I told
    you he had a sweet breath.

PINCHWIFE Write.   110

MRS PINCHWIFE Let me but put out 'loathed'.

PINCHWIFE Write, I say.

MRS PINCHWIFE Well then. [*Writes*]

PINCHWIFE Let's see, what have you writ? [*Takes the paper
    and reads*] 'Though I suffered last night your kisses   115
    and embraces' – Thou impudent creature, where is
    'nauseous' and 'loathed'?

MRS PINCHWIFE I can't abide to write such filthy words.

PINCHWIFE Once more write as I'd have you, and question
    it not, or I will spoil thy writing with this. [*Holds up*   120
    the penknife] I will stab out those eyes that cause my
    mischief.

MRS PINCHWIFE O Lord, I will!

PINCHWIFE So – so – let's see now! [*Reads*] 'Though I
    suffered last night your nauseous, loathed kisses and   125
    embraces' – go on – 'yet I would not have you presume
    that you shall ever repeat them' – So –
        [*She writes.*]

MRS PINCHWIFE I have writ it.

150   *wax and a candle:*   items used to make a seal for the envelope. The candle would melt a solid piece of wax, which would set again on the envelope once cooled.

152–3   *'For Mr Horner .'... told me his name:*   a further example of how Pinchwife inadvertently assists his wife's intrigue with Horner. See also lines 179–180.

PINCHWIFE On then. – 'I then concealed myself from your
knowledge to avoid your insolencies' –   130
    [*She writes.*]

MRS PINCHWIFE So –

PINCHWIFE 'The same reason, now I am out of your hands' –
    [*She writes.*]

MRS PINCHWIFE So –

PINCHWIFE 'Makes me own to you my unfortunate, though
innocent, frolic, of being in man's clothes' –   135
    [*She writes.*]

MRS PINCHWIFE So –

PINCHWIFE 'That you may for evermore cease to pursue
her, who hates and detests you' –
    [*She writes on.*]

MRS PINCHWIFE So – h – [*Sighs*]

PINCHWIFE What, do you sigh? – 'detests you – as much as   140
she loves her husband and her honour'.

MRS PINCHWIFE I vow, husband, he'll ne'er believe I should
write such a letter.

PINCHWIFE What, he'd expect a kinder from you? Come,
now your name only.   145

MRS PINCHWIFE What, shan't I say, 'Your most faithful,
humble servant till death'?

PINCHWIFE No, tormenting fiend! [*Aside*] Her style, I find,
would be very soft. – Come, wrap it up now, whilst I
go fetch wax and a candle, and write on the backside,   150
'For Mr Horner.'
    [*Exit* PINCHWIFE.]

MRS PINCHWIFE 'For Mr Horner.' – So, I am glad he has
told me his name. Dear Mr Horner! But why should I
send thee such a letter that will vex thee and make thee
angry with me? – Well, I will not send it – Ay, but then   155
my husband will kill me – for I see plainly he won't let
me love Mr Horner – but what care I for my husband?
– I won't, so I won't send poor Mr Horner such a

161 *shift:* stratagem, plan for effecting one's purpose

163 *presently:* immediately

166 *y'vads:* in faith

letter – But then my husband – But oh – What if I writ
at bottom, 'My husband made me write it'? – Ay, but   160
then my husband would see't – Can one have no shift?
Ah, a London woman would have had a hundred
presently. Stay – what if I should write a letter, and
wrap it up like this, and write upon't too? Ay, but then
my husband would see't – I don't know what to do –   165
But yet y'vads I'll try, so I will – for I will not send this
letter to poor Mr Horner, come what will on't.

[*She writes, and repeats what she hath writ*]
'Dear, sweet Mr Horner' – so – 'my husband would
have me send you a base, rude, unmannerly letter – but
I won't' – so – 'and would have me forbid you loving   170
me – but I won't' – so – 'and would have me say to
you, I hate you, poor Mr Horner – but I won't tell a lie
for him' – there – 'for I'm sure if you and I were in the
country at cards together' – so – 'I could not help
treading on your toe under the table' – so – 'or rubbing   175
knees with you and staring in your face till you saw
me' – very well – 'and then looking down and blushing
for an hour together' – so – 'but I must make haste
before my husband come; and now he has taught me
to write letters, you shall have longer ones from me,   180
who am,

Dear, dear, poor, dear Mr Horner,
                    Your most humble friend, and servant
                              to command till death,
                                        Margery Pinchwife.' 185
Stay, I must give him a hint at bottom – so – now wrap
it up just like t'other – so – now write, 'For Mr
Horner' – But, oh now, what shall I do with it? For
here comes my husband.

[*Enter* PINCHWIFE.]

190–92 *I have been detained ... to my wife:* another example of Pinchwife's obsessional jealousy. Do you detect any others in the scene?

196 *No, I must not give him that:* Margery almost hands Pinchwife the wrong letter; this is a verbal identification of visual 'business', that would make it quite clear to the audience that she has switched the letters.

206 *curiously:* skilfully

216–22 *At least, 'tis fit she think so ... false intelligence:* Look carefully at the imagery that Pinchwife uses here. What indication does it give you of how he sees women and marriage?

220 *frontier town:* a town built on the borders of civilisation. Pinchwife's metaphor emphasises how his wife is vulnerable to 'capture'.

PINCHWIFE [*aside*] I have been detained by a sparkish   190
    coxcomb, who pretended a visit to me; but I fear 'twas
    to my wife. – What, have you done?
MRS PINCHWIFE Ay, ay, bud, just now.
PINCHWIFE Let's see't. What d'ye tremble for? What, you
    would not have it go?   195
MRS PINCHWIFE Here. [*Aside*] No, I must not give him that;
    so I had been served if I had given him this.
PINCHWIFE [*He opens, and reads the first letter*] Come,
    where's the wax and seal?
MRS PINCHWIFE [*aside*] Lord, what shall I do now? Nay,   200
    then, I have it. – Pray let me see't. Lord, you think me
    so arrant a fool I cannot seal a letter. I will do't, so I
    will.
       [*Snatches the letter from him, changes it for the other,
       seals it and delivers it to him.*]
PINCHWIFE Nay, I believe you will learn that, and other
    things too, which I would not have you.   205
MRS PINCHWIFE So, han't I done it curiously? [*Aside*] I think
    I have; there's my letter going to Mr Horner, since he'll
    needs have me send letters to folks.
PINCHWIFE 'Tis very well; but I warrant you would not
    have it go now?   210
MRS PINCHWIFE Yes, indeed, but I would, bud, now.
PINCHWIFE Well, you are a good girl then. Come, let me
    lock you up in your chamber, till I come back, and be
    sure you come not within three strides of the window
    when I am gone, for I have a spy in the street.   215
       [*Exit* MRS PINCHWIFE. PINCHWIFE *locks the door.*]
    At least, 'tis fit she think so. If we do not cheat
    women, they'll cheat us, and fraud may be justly used
    with secret enemies, of which a wife is the most
    dangerous, and he that has a handsome one to keep,
    and a frontier town, must provide against treachery   220

222 Stage direction *(Holds up the letter):* How should Pinchwife's confidence be projected as he goes off at the end of the scene?

rather than open force. Now I have secured all within,
I'll deal with the foe without with false intelligence.
   [*Holds up the letter. Exit* PINCHWIFE.]

Act IV, Scene III

The reappearance of the Quack provides an opportunity for Horner to update the audience on the progress of his plan.

---

1 *fadges:* succeeds

2 *projectors:* schemers. The Quack's implication is that Horner's plan is a 'hare-brained scheme'.

4 *domine:* sir, master. Horner is probably being ironic.

14 *pallats:* mattresses

19 *squab:* short and plump

27 *kept:* actor or actress 'kept' as a gigolo or mistress by a wealthy patron

Act Four   Scene Three

[*The scene changes to* HORNER's *lodging.*]

[QUACK *and* HORNER.]

QUACK Well, sir, how fadges the new design? Have you
not the luck of all your brother projectors, to deceive
only yourself at last?

HORNER No, good domine doctor, I deceive you, it seems,
and others too, for the grave matrons and old, rigid   5
husbands think me as unfit for love as they are but
their wives, sisters and daughters know some of 'em
better things already.

QUACK Already!

HORNER Already, I say. Last night I was drunk with half a   10
dozen of your civil persons, as you call 'em, and people
of honour, and so was made free of their society and
dressing-rooms forever hereafter, and am already come
to the privileges of sleeping upon their pallats,
warming smocks, tying shoes and garters, and the like,   15
doctor, already, already, doctor.

QUACK You have made use of your time, sir.

HORNER I tell thee, I am now no more interruption to 'em
when they sing or talk bawdy than a little squab
French page who speaks no English.   20

QUACK But do civil persons and women of honour drink
and sing bawdy songs?

HORNER O, amongst friends, amongst friends. For your
bigots in honour are just like those in religion; they
fear the eye of the world more than the eye of Heaven   25
and think there is no virtue but railing at vice and no
sin but giving scandal. They rail at a poor, little, kept

165

28–9 *pulpit comedian:* clergyman

34 Stage direction *(Enter my Lady Fidget, looking about her):* The appearance of Lady Fidget gives Horner the chance to prove the success of his plan 'already' and also to demonstrate the hypocrisy of the 'women of honour' he describes in lines 23–30.

51 *smooty:* smutty

56 *a younger brother:* Younger brothers were traditionally very poor since elder brothers received inheritances, hence the word 'money' would be a very sore point with them.

59 *chary:* wary, cautious

player and keep themselves some young, modest pulpit
comedian to be privy to their sins in their closets, not
to tell 'em of them in their chapels.   30

QUACK Nay, the truth on't is, priests among the women
now have quite got the better of us lay confessors,
physicians.

HORNER And they are rather their patients, but –
[*Enter* MY LADY FIDGET, *looking about her.*]
Now we talk of women of honour, here comes one.   35
Step behind the screen there and but observe if I have
not particular privileges with the women of reputation
already, doctor, already.
[QUACK *steps behind screen.*]

LADY FIDGET Well, Horner, am not I a woman of honour?
You see I'm as good as my word.   40

HORNER And you shall see, madam, I'll not be behindhand
with you in honour and I'll be as good as my word
too, if you please but to withdraw into the next room.

LADY FIDGET But first, my dear sir, you must promise to
have a care of my dear honour.   45

HORNER If you talk a word more of your honour, you'll
make me incapable to wrong it. To talk of honour in
the mysteries of love is like talking of heaven or the
deity in an operation of witchcraft, just when you are
employing the devil; it makes the charm impotent.   50

LADY FIDGET Nay, fie, let us not be smooty. But you talk of
mysteries and bewitching to me; I don't understand
you.

HORNER I tell you, madam, the word 'money' in a
mistress's mouth, at such a nick of time, is not a more   55
disheartening sound to a younger brother than that of
'honour' to an eager lover like myself.

LADY FIDGET But you can't blame a lady of my reputation
to be chary.

73 *I am a Machiavel in love, madam:*   Machiavel is a shortened version of the Italian Renaissance diplomat and writer Niccolo Machiavelli who became infamous for his recommendation of treachery and deceitfulness in politics in order to justify ultimate ends. Horner's use of the term about himself is highly appropriate and self-revealing.

79 Stage direction *(Enter Sir Jaspar Fidget):*   Sir Jaspar's entrance heralds the beginning of one of the play's most infamous, and hilarious sections – 'the china scene'. It is a good example of a style of comedy known as farce and in this case involves being, or nearly being, 'caught in the act'. In Wycherley's final play, *The Plain Dealer*, one of the characters, Olivia, a deceitful, drunken and lustful woman with certain similarities to Lady Fidget, expresses her disgust at *The Country Wife* in general, but especially the 'china scene', in protest at which she breaks all her own china:
'O believe me: 'tis a filthy play and you may take my word for a filthy play as soon as another's.'

84–5 *I am trying ... were ticklish:*   trying to find out if Mr Horner is ticklish

90 *china house:*   a place where china objects were exhibited and sold and also notorious as places where assignations between lovers took place. NB china was rare and expensive.

HORNER Chary! I have been chary of it already, by the   60
report I have caused of myself.

LADY FIDGET Ay, but if you should ever let other women
know that dear secret, it would come out. Nay, you
must have a great care of your conduct, for my
acquaintance are so censorious (oh, 'tis a wicked,   65
censorious world, Mr Horner!), I say, are so
censorious and detracting that perhaps they'll talk, to
the prejudice of my honour, though you should not let
them know the dear secret.

HORNER Nay, madam, rather than they shall prejudice   70
your honour, I'll prejudice theirs, and, to serve you, I'll
lie with 'em all, make the secret their own, and then
they'll keep it. I am a Machiavel in love, madam.

LADY FIDGET Oh, no, sir, not that way.

HORNER Nay, the devil take me if censorious women are to   75
be silenced any other way.

LADY FIDGET A secret is better kept, I hope, by a single
person than a multitude; therefore pray do not trust
anybody else with it, dear, dear Mr Horner.
[*Embracing him*]
    [*Enter* SIR JASPAR FIDGET.]

SIR JASPAR How now!   80

LADY FIDGET [*aside*] Oh, my husband – prevented – and
what's almost as bad, found with my arms about
another man – that will appear too much – what shall
I say? – Sir Jaspar, come hither, I am trying if Mr
Horner were ticklish, and he's as ticklish as can be; I   85
love to torment the confounded toad. Let you and I
tickle him.

SIR JASPAR No, your ladyship will tickle him better
without me, I suppose. But is this your buying china? I
thought you had been at the china house.   90

HORNER [*aside*] China house! That's my cue, I must take
it. – A pox, can't you keep your impertinent wives at

169

95 *journeyman:*   one who labours on behalf of another, ie Horner is helping to 'entertain' Lady Fidget for Sir Jaspar

96 *drudge:*   slave

  squire: escort

97 *pies and jays:*   birds, but here fops and rakes

99 *hackney:*   hired

102 *tell:*   count

115 *he knows china very well:*   The sexual innuendo on 'china' which extends throughout the remainder of the scene begins here. There are others of a similar nature which you may spot.

home? Some men are troubled with the husbands, but
I with the wives. But I'd have you to know, since I
cannot be your journeyman by night, I will not be your   95
drudge by day, to squire your wife about and be your
man of straw, or scarecrow, only to pies and jays, that
would be nibbling at your forbidden fruit; I shall be
shortly the hackney gentleman-usher of the town.

Sir Jaspar [*aside*] Heh, heh, he! Poor fellow, he's in the   100
right on't, faith; to squire women about for other folks
is as ungrateful an employment as to tell money for
other folks. – Heh, he, he! Ben't angry, Horner –

Lady Fidget No, 'tis I have more reason to be angry, who
am left by you to go abroad indecently alone; or, what   105
is more indecent, to pin myself upon such ill-bred
people of your acquaintance as this is.

Sir Jaspar Nay, prithee, what has he done?

Lady Fidget Nay, he has done nothing.

Sir Jaspar But what d'ye take ill, if he has done nothing?   110

Lady Fidget Hah, hah, hah! Faith, I can't but laugh,
however; why d'ye think the unmannerly toad would
not come down to me to the coach? I was fain to come
up to fetch him, or go without him, which I was
resolved not to do, for he knows china very well and   115
has himself very good, but will not let me see it lest I
should beg some. But I will find it out and have what I
came for yet.

　　[*Exit* LADY FIDGET *and locks the door, followed by*
　　HORNER *to the door.*]

Horner [*apart to* LADY FIDGET] Lock the door, madam.
– So, she has got into my chamber, and locked me out.   120
Oh, the impertinency of womankind! Well, Sir Jaspar,
plain-dealing is a jewel; if ever you suffer your wife to
trouble me again here, she shall carry you home a pair
of horns, by my Lord Mayor she shall;

140–45 Compare Sir Jaspar's position here with Pinchwife's during Act IV.

147–8 Should the Quack be visible to the audience throughout this scene, or only now when required to speak? How is the effect different in each case?

though I cannot furnish you myself, you are sure, yet   125
I'll find a way.

SIR JASPAR [*aside*] Hah, ha, he! At my first coming in and
finding her arms about him, tickling him it seems, I
was half jealous, but now I see my folly. – Heh, he, he!
Poor Horner.   130

HORNER Nay, though you laugh now, 'twill be my turn ere
long. Oh, women, more impertinent, more cunning
and more mischievous than their monkeys, and to me
almost as ugly! Now is she throwing my things about
and rifling all I have, but I'll get into her the back way   135
and so rifle her for it.

SIR JASPAR Hah, ha, ha, poor angry Horner.

HORNER Stay here a little; I'll ferret her out to you
presently, I warrant.

[*Exit* HORNER *at t'other door.*]

SIR JASPAR Wife! My Lady Fidget! Wife! He is coming into   140
you the back way.

[SIR JASPAR *calls through the door to his wife; she
answers from within.*]

LADY FIDGET Let him come, and welcome, which way he
will.

SIR JASPAR He'll catch you and use you roughly and be too
strong for you.   145

LADY FIDGET Don't you trouble yourself; let him if he can.

QUACK [*behind*] This indeed I could not have believed
from him, nor any but my own eyes.

[*Enter* MRS SQUEAMISH.]

SQUEAMISH Where's this woman-hater, this toad, this ugly,
greasy, dirty sloven?   150

SIR JASPAR [*aside*] So, the women all will have him ugly;
methinks he is a comely person, but his wants make
his form contemptible to 'em and 'tis e'en as my wife
said yesterday, talking of him, that a proper handsome
eunuch was as ridiculous a thing as a gigantic coward.   155

159 *playing the wag:* literally, having a joke with. It functions here, too, as a fairly obvious sexual innuendo.

170 *tomrig:* Literally tomboy, but the meaning is closer to strumpet or tart.

171 *vild:* vile or disgraceful

SQUEAMISH Sir Jaspar, your servant. Where is the odious beast?

SIR JASPAR He's within in his chamber, with my wife; she's playing the wag with him.

SQUEAMISH Is she so? And he's a clownish beast, he'll give her no quarter; he'll play the wag with her again, let me tell you. Come, let's go help her. – What, the door's locked? 160

SIR JASPAR Ay, my wife locked it.

SQUEAMISH Did she so? Let us break it open then. 165

SIR JASPAR No, no, he'll do her no hurt.

SQUEAMISH No. [*Aside*] But is there no other way to get in to 'em? Whither goes this? I will disturb 'em.
[*Exit* SQUEAMISH *at another door.*]
[*Enter* OLD LADY SQUEAMISH.]

OLD LADY SQUEAMISH Where is this harlotry, this impudent baggage, this rambling tomrig? O Sir Jaspar, I'm glad to see you here. Did you not see my vild grandchild come in hither just now? 170

SIR JASPAR Yes.

OLD LADY SQUEAMISH Ay, but where is she then? Where is she? Lord, Sir Jaspar, I have e'en rattled myself to pieces in pursuit of her. But can you tell what she makes here? They say below, no woman lodges here. 175

SIR JASPAR No.

OLD LADY SQUEAMISH No! What does she here then? Say, if it be not a woman's lodging, what makes she here? But are you sure no woman lodges here? 180

SIR JASPAR No, nor no man neither; this is Mr Horner's lodging.

OLD LADY SQUEAMISH Is it so, are you sure?

SIR JASPAR Yes, yes. 185

OLD LADY SQUEAMISH So then there's no hurt in't, I hope. But where is he?

SIR JASPAR He's in the next room with my wife.

175

191–2 *as harmless a man as ever came out of Italy:* a man with a castrato voice in Italian opera, a voice associated with eunuchs

198 Stage direction *(Enter Lady Fidget with a piece of china in her hand, and Horner following.):* potentially, a great comic entrance. How do you imagine they look when they appear?

199 *moiling:* labouring

218 *roll-wagon:* a phallic-shaped cylindrical vase

OLD LADY SQUEAMISH Nay, if you trust him with your wife, I
    may with my Biddy. They say he's a merry harmless   190
    man now, e'en as harmless a man as ever came out of
    Italy with a good voice, and as pretty harmless
    company for a lady as a snake without his teeth.
SIR JASPAR Ay, ay, poor man.
        [*Enter* MRS SQUEAMISH.]
SQUEAMISH I can't find 'em. – Oh, are you here,   195
    Grandmother? I followed, you must know, my Lady
    Fidget hither; 'tis the prettiest lodging and I have been
    staring on the prettiest pictures.
        [*Enter* LADY FIDGET *with a piece of china in her hand,
        and* HORNER *following.*]
LADY FIDGET And I have been toiling and moiling for the
    prettiest piece of china, my dear.   200
HORNER Nay, she has been too hard for me, do what I
    could.
SQUEAMISH O Lord, I'll have some china too. Good Mr
    Horner, don't think to give other people china and me
    none; come in with me too.   205
HORNER Upon my honour, I have none left now.
SQUEAMISH Nay, nay, I have known you deny your china
    before now, but you shan't put me off so. Come –
HORNER This lady had the last there.
LADY FIDGET Yes, indeed, madam, to my certain knowledge 210
    he has no more left.
SQUEAMISH O, but it may be he may have some you could
    not find.
LADY FIDGET What, d'ye think if he had had any left, I
    would not have had it too? For we women of quality   215
    never think we have china enough.
HORNER Do not take it ill. I cannot make china for you all,
    but I will have a roll-wagon for you too, another time.
SQUEAMISH Thank you, dear toad.

177

234 *sloven:*   a lazy, dirty or badly dressed person

236 *nice:*   fastidious or fussy

242 *picture in little:*   miniature painting, very popular during the Restoration

LADY FIDGET [*to* HORNER *aside*] What do you mean by   220
    that promise?
HORNER [*apart to* LADY FIDGET] Alas, she has an
    innocent, literal understanding.
OLD LADY SQUEAMISH Poor Mr Horner, he has enough to do
    to please you all, I see.   225
HORNER Ay, madam, you see how they use me.
OLD LADY SQUEAMISH Poor gentleman, I pity you.
HORNER I thank you, madam. I could never find pity but
    from such reverend ladies as you are; the young ones
    will never spare a man.   230
SQUEAMISH Come, come, beast, and go dine with us, for
    we shall want a man at ombre after dinner.
HORNER That's all their use of me, madam, you see.
SQUEAMISH Come, sloven, I'll lead you, to be sure of you.
    [*Pulls him by the cravat*]
OLD LADY SQUEAMISH Alas, poor man, how she tugs him!   235
    Kiss, kiss her; that's the way to make such nice women
    quiet.
HORNER No, madam, that remedy is worse than the
    torment; they know I dare suffer anything rather than
    do it.   240
OLD LADY SQUEAMISH Prithee, kiss her and I'll give you her
    picture in little, that you admired so last night; prithee
    do.
HORNER Well, nothing but that could bribe me; I love a
    woman only in effigy and good painting, as much as I   245
    hate them. I'll do't, for I could adore the devil well
    painted. [*Kisses* MRS SQUEAMISH]
SQUEAMISH Foh, you filthy toad! Nay, now I've done
    jesting.
OLD LADY SQUEAMISH Ha, ha, ha, I told you so.   250
SQUEAMISH Foh, a kiss of his –
SIR JASPAR Has no more hurt in't than one of my spaniel's.
SQUEAMISH Nor no more good neither.

255–62 The near-hysterical reactions of the ladies as they flee from Horner's chamber expose their hypocrisy.

273 *diffide in:* distrust

279 *second:* supporter, a term derived from the practice of duelling

281 *grum:* bad-tempered (as in 'grumpy')

282 *strange to me:* treating him as one would a stranger

QUACK [*behind*] I will now believe anything he tells me.
 [*Enter* MR PINCHWIFE.]

LADY FIDGET O Lord, here's a man! Sir Jaspar, my mask,   255
 my mask! I would not be seen here for the world.

SIR JASPAR What, not when I am with you?

LADY FIDGET No, no, my honour – let's be gone.

SQUEAMISH Oh, Grandmother, let us be gone; make haste,
 make haste, I know not how he may censure us.   260

LADY FIDGET Be found in the lodging of anything like a
 man! Away!
  [*Exeunt* SIR JASPAR, LADY FIDGET, OLD LADY
  SQUEAMISH, MRS SQUEAMISH.]

QUACK [*behind*] What's here? Another cuckold? He looks
 like one, and none else sure have any business with
 him.   265

HORNER Well, what brings my dear friend hither?

PINCHWIFE Your impertinency.

HORNER My impertinency! – Why, you gentlemen that
 have got handsome wives think you have a privilege of
 saying anything to your friends and are as brutish as if 270
 you were our creditors.

PINCHWIFE No, sir, I'll ne'er trust you any way.

HORNER But why not, dear Jack? Why diffide in me thou
 knowest so well?

PINCHWIFE Because I do know you so well.   275

HORNER Han't I been always thy friend, honest Jack,
 always ready to serve thee, in love or battle, before
 thou wert married, and am so still?

PINCHWIFE I believe so; you would be my second now
 indeed.   280

HORNER Well then, dear Jack, why so unkind, so grum, so
 strange to me? Come, prithee kiss me, dear rogue.
 Gad, I was always, I say, and am still as much thy
 servant as –

291–2 *Lombard Street ... Locket's:* Lombard Street was famous for its goldsmiths and hence is associated with wealth. Locket's was a fashionable and expensive restaurant near Charing Cross. The rather obscure point is, presumably, that the rich man, who may be a moneylender too, is suspicious of receiving courtesy since he may think a gentleman is about to default on paying his debts. Pinchwife, according to Horner, is being unnecessarily cautious.

304 Horner would be genuinely surprised, even confused, by this. How should this be communicated to the audience but not to Pinchwife?

315 *or kill my squirrel:* This line traditionally receives one of the biggest laughs in performance. Why do you think this is? Would a modern audience be laughing for the same reason as the Restoration audience?

PINCHWIFE As I am yours, sir. What, you would send a kiss   285
to my wife, is that it?

HORNER So, there 'tis – a man can't show his friendship to
a married man but presently he talks of his wife to
you. Prithee, let thy wife alone and let thee and I be all
one, as we were wont. What, thou art as shy of my   290
kindness as a Lombard Street alderman of a courtier's
civility at Locket's.

PINCHWIFE But you are overkind to me, as kind as if I were
your cuckold already; yet I must confess you ought to
be kind and civil to me, since I am so kind, so civil to   295
you, as to bring you this. Look you there, sir. [*Delivers
him a letter*]

HORNER What is't?

PINCHWIFE Only a love-letter, sir.

HORNER From whom? – how! this is from your wife – hum
– and hum – [*Reads*]   300

PINCHWIFE Even from my wife, sir. Am I not wondrous
kind and civil to you now too? [*Aside*] But you'll not
think her so.

HORNER [*aside*] Ha, is this a trick of his or hers?

PINCHWIFE The gentleman's surprised, I find. What, you   305
expected a kinder letter?

HORNER No, faith, not I, how could I?

PINCHWIFE Yes, yes, I'm sure you did; a man so well made
as you are must needs be disappointed if the women
declare not their passion at first sight or opportunity.   310

HORNER [*aside*] But what should this mean? Stay, the
postscript. [*Reads aside*] 'Be sure you love me,
whatsoever my husband says to the contrary, and let
him not see this, lest he should come home and pinch
me, or kill my squirrel.' [*Aside*] It seems he knows not   315
what the letter contains.

PINCHWIFE Come, ne'er wonder at it so much.

HORNER Faith, I can't help it.

183

337 *of thy last clap:*   your last bout of sexually transmitted disease

338 The ability to wear a sword in a gentlemanly and elegant way was a high point of Restoration fashion: it was very easy to make a fool of yourself or damage yourself with it.

346 *design:*   plan to do

352 How does Pinchwife deliver this line?

PINCHWIFE Now, I think, I have deserved your infinite
     friendship and kindness and have showed myself   320
     sufficiently an obliging kind friend and husband; am I
     not so, to bring a letter from my wife to her gallant?
HORNER Ay, the devil take me, art thou the most obliging,
     kind friend and husband in the world, ha, ha!
PINCHWIFE Well, you may be merry, sir; but in short I must   325
     tell you, sir, my honour will suffer no jesting.
HORNER What dost thou mean?
PINCHWIFE Does the letter want a comment? Then know,
     sir, though I have been so civil a husband as to bring
     you a letter from my wife, to let you kiss and court her   330
     to my face, I will not be a cuckold, sir, I will not.
HORNER Thou art mad with jealousy. I never saw thy wife
     in my life but at the play yesterday, and I know not if
     it were she or no. I court her, kiss her!
PINCHWIFE I will not be a cuckold, I say; there will be   335
     danger in making me a cuckold.
HORNER Why, wert thou not well cured of thy last clap?
PINCHWIFE I wear a sword.
HORNER It should be taken from thee lest thou shouldst do
     thyself a mischief with it; thou art mad, man.   340
PINCHWIFE As mad as I am, and as merry as you are, I must
     have more reason from you ere we part. I say again,
     though you kissed and courted last night my wife in
     man's clothes, as she confesses in her letter –
HORNER [aside] Ha!   345
PINCHWIFE Both she and I say, you must not design it
     again, for you have mistaken your woman, as you
     have done your man.
HORNER [aside] Oh – I understand something now. – Was
     that thy wife? Why wouldst thou not tell me 'twas she?   350
     Faith, my freedom with her was your fault, not mine.
PINCHWIFE [aside] Faith, so 'twas.

359 *you see by her letter …:*   Again, Pinchwife's misplaced self-confidence, here, is very similar to that of Sir Jaspar's in encouraging Horner to escort his wife.

370 *tittle:*   in the smallest detail

384 *original:*   unusual

HORNER Fie, I'd never do't to a woman before her
husband's face, sure.

PINCHWIFE But I had rather you should do't to my wife   355
before my face than behind my back, and that you
shall never do.

HORNER No – you will hinder me.

PINCHWIFE If I would not hinder you, you see by her letter,
she would.   360

HORNER Well, I must e'en acquiesce then and be contented
with what she writes.

PINCHWIFE I'll assure you 'twas voluntarily writ; I had no
hand in't, you may believe me.

HORNER I do believe thee, faith.   365

PINCHWIFE And believe her too, for she's an innocent
creature, has no dissembling in her; and so fare you
well, sir.

HORNER Pray, however, present my humble service to her
and tell her I will obey her letter to a tittle and fulfil   370
her desires, be what they will, or with what difficulty
soever I do't, and you shall be no more jealous of me, I
warrant her and you.

PINCHWIFE Well, then, fare you well, and play with any
man's honour but mine, kiss any man's wife but mine,   375
and welcome.

　　　[*Exit* MR PINCHWIFE.]

HORNER Ha, ha, ha, doctor.

QUACK It seems he has not heard the report of you, or
does not believe it.

HORNER Ha, ha! Now, doctor, what think you?   380

QUACK Pray let's see the letter – hum – [*Reads the letter*]
'for – dear – love you – '

HORNER I wonder how she could contrive it! What say'st
thou to't? 'Tis an original.

QUACK So are your cuckolds, too, originals, for they are   385
like no other common cuckolds, and I will henceforth

387–8 *Grand Signior:*   the person in charge of a Turkish harem

389–91 What is Horner's opinion of the letter? What makes the letter so unusual?

399 *Common Prayer:*   standard part of the marriage service

404 *Piazza:*   open arcade of two sides of Covent Garden, designed by Inigo Jones in the early part of the seventeenth century

410 Pinchwife's observation, albeit inaccurate, is important to the plot in the next scene (see also lines 419–420).

believe it not impossible for you to cuckold the Grand
Signior amidst his guards of eunuchs, that I say.

HORNER And I say for the letter, 'tis the first love-letter
that ever was without flames, darts, fates, destinies,   390
lying and dissembling in't.

[*Enter* SPARKISH, *pulling in* MR PINCHWIFE.]

SPARKISH Come back, you are a pretty brother-in-law,
neither go to church, nor to dinner with your sister
bride!

PINCHWIFE My sister denies her marriage and you see is   395
gone away from you dissatisfied.

SPARKISH Pshaw, upon a foolish scruple, that our parson
was not in lawful orders and did not say all the
Common Prayer; but 'tis her modesty only, I believe.
But let women be never so modest the first day, they'll   400
be sure to come to themselves by night, and I shall
have enough of her then. In the meantime, Harry
Horner, you must dine with me; I keep my wedding at
my aunt's in the Piazza.

HORNER Thy wedding! What stale maid has lived to   405
despair of a husband, or what young one of a gallant?

SPARKISH Oh, your servant, sir – this gentleman's sister
then – no stale maid.

HORNER I'm sorry for't.

PINCHWIFE [*aside*] How comes he so concerned for her?   410

SPARKISH You sorry for't? Why, do you know any ill by
her?

HORNER No, I know none but by thee; 'tis for her sake,
not yours, and another man's sake that might have
hoped, I thought.   415

SPARKISH Another man, another man! What is his name?

HORNER Nay, since 'tis past he shall be nameless. [*Aside*]
Poor Harcourt, I am sorry thou hast missed her.

PINCHWIFE [*aside*] He seems to be much troubled at the
match.   420

189

429 *orange to veal:* Orange sauce is a traditional accompaniment to a dish of veal.

440 *firkin:* cask

442 *smack:* taste

443 *dust it away:* 'polish it off'

Sparkish Prithee tell me – nay, you shan't go, brother.

Pinchwife I must of necessity, but I'll come to you to dinner.

[*Exit* PINCHWIFE.]

Sparkish But, Harry, what, have I a rival in my wife already? But with all my heart, for he may be of use to me hereafter, for though my hunger is now my sauce and I can fall on heartily without, but the time will come when a rival will be as good sauce for a married man to a wife as an orange to veal. 425

Horner O thou damned rogue! Thou hast set my teeth on edge with thy orange. 430

Sparkish Then let's to dinner – there I was with you again. Come.

Horner But who dines with thee?

Sparkish My friends and relations, my brother Pinchwife, you see, of your acquaintance. 435

Horner And his wife?

Sparkish No, gad, he'll ne'er let her come amongst us good fellows. Your stingy country coxcomb keeps his wife from his friends, as he does his little firkin of ale for his own drinking, and a gentleman can't get a smack on't; but his servants, when his back is turned, broach it at their pleasures and dust it away, ha, ha, ha! Gad, I am witty, I think, considering I was married today, by the world. But come – 440

445

Horner No, I will not dine with you, unless you can fetch her too.

Sparkish Pshaw, what pleasure canst thou have with women now, Harry?

Horner My eyes are not gone; I love a good prospect yet and will not dine with you unless she does too. Go fetch her, therefore, but do not tell her husband 'tis for my sake. 450

457–9 A true act of heroism or a parody of it? How do you interpret the tone of these lines?

458–9 *over the pale:* over the fence, out of trouble

Sparkish Well, I'll go try what I can do. In the meantime come away to my aunt's lodging; 'tis in the way to   455
Pinchwife's.

Horner The poor woman has called for aid and stretched forth her hand, doctor; I cannot but help her over the pale out of the briars.

    [*Exeunt* SPARKISH, HORNER, QUACK.]

Act IV, Scene IV

1–14 How is Wycherley trying to influence your attitude to, and feelings for, Margery in this speech?

4 *ague:* fever

9 *fain:* rather

14 *sick, sick:* lovesick, or sick at heart

16 Stage direction *(offers):* attempts

17 *stir:* leave

20–34 What do you find comic in the style of Margery's latest letter to Horner?

Act Four   Scene Four

[*The scene changes to* PINCHWIFE'*s house.*]

[MRS PINCHWIFE *alone, leaning on her elbow. A table, pen, ink and paper.*]

Mrs Pinchwife Well, 'tis e'en so, I have got the London
disease they call love; I am sick of my husband and for
my gallant. I have heard this distemper called a fever,
but methinks 'tis liker an ague, for when I think of my
husband, I tremble and am in a cold sweat and have   5
inclinations to vomit, but when I think of my gallant,
dear Mr Horner, my hot fit comes and I am all in a
fever, indeed, and as in other fevers my own chamber
is tedious to me and I would fain be removed to his
and then methinks I should be well. Ah, poor Mr   10
Horner! Well, I cannot, will not stay here; therefore I'd
make an end of my letter to him, which shall be a finer
letter than my last, because I have studied it like
anything. O, sick, sick! [*Takes the pen and writes*]
  [*Enter* MR PINCHWIFE, *who, seeing her writing, steals
  softly behind her and, looking over her shoulder, snatches
  the paper from her.*]
Pinchwife What, writing more letters?   15
Mrs Pinchwife O Lord, bud, why d'ye fright me so?
  [*She offers to run out; he stops her and reads.*]
Pinchwife How's this! Nay, you shall not stir, madam.
  'Dear, dear, dear Mr Horner' – very well – I have taught
  you to write letters to good purpose – but let's see't.
  'First, I am to beg your pardon for my boldness in   20
  writing to you, which I'd have you to know I would
  not have done had not you said first you loved me so

195

27–9 *this unfortunate match ... my choice:* What serious point about marriage is being made here that has not previously been raised?

36 *love:* personified

41 *dough-baked:* half-baked, foolish

42 *politic:* wise, sensible

46 *passionate:* hot-tempered

51 *drawn upon:* obscene pun (developed in line 52)

extremely, which if you do, you will never suffer me to
lie in the arms of another man, whom I loathe,
nauseate and detest.' – Now you can write these filthy   25
words. But what follows? – 'Therefore I hope you will
speedily find some way to free me from this
unfortunate match, which was never, I assure you, of
my choice, but I'm afraid 'tis already too far gone.
However, if you love me, as I do you, you will try   30
what you can do, but you must help me away before
tomorrow, or else, alas, I shall be forever out of your
reach, for I can defer no longer our – our' [*The letter
concludes*] – What is to follow 'our'? – Speak, what?
Our journey into the country, I suppose – Oh, woman,   35
damned woman and love, damned love, their old
tempter! For this is one of his miracles; in a moment he
can make all those blind that could see and those see
that were blind, those dumb that could speak and
those prattle who were dumb before; nay, what is   40
more than all, make these dough-baked, senseless,
indocile animals, women, too hard for us, their politic
lords and rulers, in a moment. But make an end of
your letter and then I'll make an end of you thus, and
all my plagues together. [*Draws his sword*]   45
MRS PINCHWIFE O Lord, O Lord, you are such a passionate
    man, bud!
    [*Enter* SPARKISH.]
SPARKISH How now, what's here to do?
PINCHWIFE This fool here now!   50
SPARKISH What, drawn upon your wife? You should never
    do that but at night in the dark, when you can't hurt
    her. This is my sister-in-law, is it not? [*Pulls aside her
    handkerchief*] Ay, faith, e'en our country Margery; one
    may know her. Come, she and you must go dine with   55
    me; dinner's ready, come. But where's my wife? Is she
    not come home yet? Where is she?

61 *cully:* dupe, cuckold

66 *wag:* stir

67 *sensible:* painfully felt

76–82 A rare glimpse of wit from a fool?

76 *shy:* suspicious

90 *breeds for:* grows cuckold's horns on her behalf

PINCHWIFE Making you a cuckold; 'tis that they all do, as
    soon as they can.

SPARKISH What, the wedding day? No, a wife that designs   60
    to make a cully of her husband will be sure to let him
    win the first stake of love, by the world. But come,
    they stay dinner for us. Come, I'll lead down our
    Margery.

PINCHWIFE No – sir, go, we'll follow you.   65

SPARKISH I will not wag without you.

PINCHWIFE [aside] This coxcomb is a sensible torment to
    me amidst the greatest in the world.

SPARKISH Come, come, Madam Margery.

PINCHWIFE No, I'll lead her my way. What, would you treat   70
    your friends with mine, for want of your own wife?
        [Leads her to t'other door and locks her in and returns.
        Aside]
    I am contented my rage should take breath.

SPARKISH [aside] I told Horner this.

PINCHWIFE Come now.   75

SPARKISH Lord, how shy you are of your wife! But let me
    tell you, brother, we men of wit have amongst us a
    saying that cuckolding, like the smallpox, comes with
    a fear, and you may keep your wife as much as you
    will out of danger of infection but if her constitution   80
    incline her to't, she'll have it sooner or later, by the
    world, say they.

PINCHWIFE [aside] What a thing is a cuckold, that every
    fool can make him ridiculous! – Well, sir – but let me
    advise you, now you are come to be concerned,   85
    because you suspect the danger, not to neglect the
    means to prevent it, especially when the greatest share
    of the malady will light upon your own head, for –
    Hows'e'er the kind wife's belly comes to swell,
    The husband breeds for her and first is ill.   90
        [Exeunt PINCHWIFE and SPARKISH.]

Act V, Scene I

The opening scene of Act V offers further evidence of Margery's growing facility to carry off stratagems even if they are not entirely of her invention, as she pretends a letter she has written to Horner is from Alithea. This, conveniently, confirms Pinchwife's suspicions aroused in Act IV, Scene III.

---

2 *false in a tittle:* lie in the smallest detail

7 *defer:* delay

9 *Must all out:* must all be revealed

12 *slighted:* snubbed because of rejection

Act Five Scene One

[MR PINCHWIFE's *house.*]

[*Enter* MR PINCHWIFE *and* MRS PINCHWIFE. *A table and candle.*]

PINCHWIFE Come, take the pen and make an end of the
letter, just as you intended; if you are false in a tittle, I
shall soon perceive it and punish you with this as you
deserve. [*Lays his hand on his sword*] Write what was
to follow – let's see – 'You must make haste and help   5
me away before tomorrow, or else I shall be forever
out of your reach, for I can defer no longer our – '
What follows 'our'?

MRS PINCHWIFE Must all out then, bud?
[MRS PINCHWIFE *takes the pen and writes*]
Look you there then.   10

PINCHWIFE Let's see – 'For I can defer no longer our –
wedding – Your slighted Alithea.' – What's the
meaning of this? My sister's name to't. Speak, unriddle!

MRS PINCHWIFE Yes, indeed, bud.

PINCHWIFE But why her name to't? Speak – speak, I say!   15

MRS PINCHWIFE Ay, but you'll tell her then again; if you
would not tell her again –

PINCHWIFE I will not – I am stunned, my head turns round.
Speak.

MRS PINCHWIFE Won't you tell her, indeed, and indeed?   20

PINCHWIFE No, speak, I say.

MRS PINCHWIFE She'll be angry with me, but I had rather
she should be angry with me than you, bud; and to tell
you the truth, 'twas she made me write the letter and
taught me what I should write.   25

201

35 *lest:* in case
Margery's ingenuity is pushed to the limit here, but she comes through the test.

46 *hark you:* listen

49 *Alackaday:* unfortunately (expressed with more feeling)

53 *discover me:* expose me

PINCHWIFE [*aside*] Ha! I thought the style was somewhat
better than her own. – But how could she come to you
to teach you, since I had locked you up alone?

MRS PINCHWIFE O, through the keyhole, bud.

PINCHWIFE But why should she make you write a letter for   30
her to him, since she can write herself?

MRS PINCHWIFE Why, she said because – for I was unwilling
to do it.

PINCHWIFE Because what – because?

MRS PINCHWIFE Because, lest Mr Horner should be cruel   35
and refuse her or vain afterwards and show the letter,
she might disown it, the hand not being hers.

PINCHWIFE [*aside*] How's this? Ha! – then I think I shall
come to myself again. This changeling could not invent
this lie; but if she could, why should she? She might   40
think I should soon discover it – stay – now I think
on't too, Horner said he was sorry she had married
Sparkish, and her disowning her marriage to me makes
me think she has evaded it for Horner's sake. Yet why
should she take this course? But men in love are fools;   45
women may well be so. – But hark you, madam, your
sister went out in the morning and I have not seen her
within since.

MRS PINCHWIFE Alackaday, she has been crying all day
above, it seems, in a corner.   50

PINCHWIFE Where is she? Let me speak with her.

MRS PINCHWIFE [*aside*] O Lord, then he'll discover all! –
Pray hold, bud. What, d'ye mean to discover me?
She'll know I have told you then. Pray, bud, let me talk
with her first.   55

PINCHWIFE I must speak with her, to know whether Horner
ever made her any promise and whether she be
married to Sparkish or no.

65–8 Notice how Margery's difficulties with lying are practical, not moral, as is Pinchwife's preference for Horner over Sparkish (ll. 69–73 and 86–89).

71 *pretensions:* sexual advances

86 *extraction:* family background

87 *his parts:* his abilities. There is an irony here since the audience, and Margery, know that Horner's 'parts' in the sexual sense are functioning perfectly, whereas Pinchwife is apparently the only man not to have heard the false rumour of Horner's impotence.

MRS PINCHWIFE Pray, dear bud, don't, till I have spoken
with her and told her that I have told you all, for she'll   60
kill me else.

PINCHWIFE Go then, and bid her come out to me.

MRS PINCHWIFE Yes, yes, bud.

PINCHWIFE Let me see –

MRS PINCHWIFE [*aside*] I'll go, but she is not within to come   65
to him. I have just got time to know of Lucy her maid,
who first set me on work, what lie I shall tell next, for
I am e'en at my wit's end.

    [*Exit* MRS PINCHWIFE.]

PINCHWIFE Well, I resolve it; Horner shall have her. I'd
rather give him my sister than lend him my wife and   70
such an alliance will prevent his pretensions to my
wife, sure. I'll make him of kin to her and then he
won't care for her.

    [MRS PINCHWIFE *returns.*]

MRS PINCHWIFE O Lord, bud, I told you what anger you
would make me with my sister.   75

PINCHWIFE Won't she come hither?

MRS PINCHWIFE No, no, alackaday, she's ashamed to look
you in the face, and she says, if you go in to her, she'll
run away downstairs and shamefully go herself to Mr
Horner, who has promised her marriage, she says, and   80
she will have no other, so she won't!

PINCHWIFE Did he so – promise her marriage – then she
shall have no other. Go tell her so, and if she will come
and discourse with me a little concerning the means, I
will about it immediately. Go.   85

    [*Exit* MRS PINCHWIFE.]

His estate is equal to Sparkish's, and his extraction as
much better than his as his parts are; but my chief
reason is, I'd rather be of kin to him by the name of
brother-in-law than that of cuckold.

    [*Enter* MRS PINCHWIFE.]

91–100 Can you detect Margery's plan at this point?

111 *free education:* Pinchwife is here complaining of how Margery has freely been able to discover 'the pleasures of the town'.

117 Stage direction *(nightgown):* a loose gown but not the same as a nightdress. Occasionally they would have been worn outdoors.

Well, what says she now?   90

MRS PINCHWIFE Why, she says she would only have you
lead her to Horner's lodging – with whom she first will
discourse the matter before she talk with you, which
yet she cannot do, for alack, poor creature, she says
she can't so much as look you in the face, therefore   95
she'll come to you in a mask, and you must excuse her
if she make you no answer to any question of yours,
till you have brought her to Mr Horner, and if you will
not chide her, nor question her, she'll come out to you
immediately.   100

PINCHWIFE Let her come. I will not speak a word to her,
nor require a word from her.

MRS PINCHWIFE Oh, I forgot; besides, she says, she cannot
look you in the face though through a mask, therefore
would desire you to put out the candle.   105

PINCHWIFE I agree to all; let her make haste – there, 'tis out.
      [*Puts out the candle*]
      [*Exit* MRS PINCHWIFE.]
My case is something better. I'd rather fight with
Horner for not lying with my sister than for lying with
my wife, and of the two I had rather find my sister too
forward than my wife; I expected no other from her   110
free education, as she calls it, and her passion for the
town. Well – wife and sister are names which make us
expect love and duty, pleasure and comfort, but we
find 'em plagues and torments, and are equally, though
differently, troublesome to their keeper, for we have as   115
much ado to get people to lie with our sisters as to
keep 'em from lying with our wives.
      [*Enter* MRS PINCHWIFE *masked and in hoods and
      scarves, and a nightgown and petticoat of* ALITHEA's, *in
      the dark.*]
What, are you come, sister? Let us go then – but first
let me lock up my wife. – Mrs Margery, where are you?

122 Stage direction: This is one of the most extravagant visual deceptions in the play. On the original Restoration stage, the only indication that it was 'in the dark' (stage direction, line 117) would be that Margery would probably carry a lantern or a candle: the facility to quickly dim the stage lights was not possible since it would have been lit by candles.

for his sister Alithea: ie, as if she were Alithea

MRS PINCHWIFE Here, bud. 120

PINCHWIFE Come hither, that I may lock you up; get you in.

　　[*Locks the door*]

　Come, sister, where are you now?

　　[MRS PINCHWIFE *gives him her hand but, when he lets*
　　her go, she steals softly on t'other side of him, and is led
　　away by him for his sister ALITHEA.]

Act V, Scene II

12–15 a further comment on the relationship between town and country

20 *cracked his credit:*   used up all his resources and influence

26 *bit:* tricked

coy: unaware

Act Five Scene Two

[The scene changes to HORNER's *lodging.]*

[QUACK, HORNER]

QUACK What, all alone? Not so much as one of your
    cuckolds here, nor one of their wives! They use to take
    their turns with you, as if they were to watch you.
HORNER Yes, it often happens that a cuckold is but his
    wife's spy and is more upon family duty when he is   5
    with her gallant abroad, hindering his pleasure, than
    when he is at home with her, playing the gallant. But
    the hardest duty a married woman imposes upon a
    lover is keeping her husband company always.
QUACK And his fondness wearies you almost as soon as   10
    hers.
HORNER A pox, keeping a cuckold company, after you
    have had his wife, is as tiresome as the company of a
    country squire to a witty fellow of the town, when he
    has got all his money.   15
QUACK And as at first a man makes a friend of the
    husband to get the wife, so at last you are fain to fall
    out with the wife to be rid of the husband.
HORNER Ay, most cuckold-makers are true courtiers; when
    once a poor man has cracked his credit for 'em, they   20
    can't abide to come near him.
QUACK But at first, to draw him in, are so sweet, so kind,
    so dear, just as you are to Pinchwife. But what
    becomes of that intrigue with his wife?
HORNER A pox, he's as surly as an alderman that has been   25
    bit and, since he's so coy, his wife's kindness is in vain,
    for she's a silly innocent.

38 How should the scene be directed so that the Quack *immediately* recognises Margery, even though her husband is still in ignorance?

41–3 Pinchwife could not have expressed the irony of his actions more clearly!

49 *usual question:*   the only issue to trouble a man

50 *sound:*   free from sexually transmitted disease

53 *paw:*   naughty, improper

QUACK Did she not send you a letter by him?

HORNER Yes, but that's a riddle I have not yet solved.
Allow the poor creature to be willing, she is silly too,   30
and he keeps her up so close –

QUACK Yes, so close that he makes her but the more
willing and adds but revenge to her love, which two,
when met, seldom fail of satisfying each other one way
or other.   35

HORNER What, here's the man we are talking of, I think.
    [*Enter* MR PINCHWIFE, *leading in his wife masked,*
    muffled and in her sister's gown.]
Pshaw!

QUACK Bringing his wife to you is the next thing to
bringing a love-letter from her.

HORNER What means this?   40

PINCHWIFE The last time, you know, sir, I brought you a
love-letter; now, you see, a mistress. I think you'll say I
am a civil man to you.

HORNER Ay, the devil take me, will I say thou art the
civilest man I ever met with, and I have known some! I   45
fancy I understand thee now better than I did the
letter. But hark thee, in thy ear –

PINCHWIFE What?

HORNER Nothing but the usual question, man: is she
sound, on thy word?   50

PINCHWIFE What, you take her for a wench and me for a
pimp?

HORNER Pshaw, wench and pimp, paw words. I know
thou art an honest fellow and hast a great
acquaintance among the ladies and perhaps hast made   55
love for me rather than let me make love to thy wife –

PINCHWIFE Come, sir, in short, I am for no fooling.

HORNER Nor I neither; therefore, prithee, let's see her face
presently. Make her show, man. Art thou sure I don't
know her?   60

71 *Do you speak to her:* speak to her. Pinchwife is *telling* Horner to speak to her, not asking him a question.

79 *if not, you and I shan't agree:* If you don't accept her as your wife, there will be conflict between us.

86 *usurers:* moneylenders

87 *put out:* in public

writings: deeds, documents

PINCHWIFE I am sure you do know her.

HORNER A pox, why dost thou bring her to me then?

PINCHWIFE Because she's a relation of mine –

HORNER Is she, faith, man? Then thou art still more civil
    and obliging, dear rogue.   65

PINCHWIFE Who desired me to bring her to you.

HORNER Then she is obliging, dear rogue.

PINCHWIFE You'll make her welcome for my sake, I hope.

HORNER I hope she is handsome enough to make herself
    welcome. Prithee, let her unmask.   70

PINCHWIFE Do you speak to her; she would never be ruled
    by me.

HORNER Madam –
    [MRS PINCHWIFE *whispers to* HORNER.]
    She says she must speak with me in private. Withdraw,
    prithee.   75

PINCHWIFE [*aside*] She's unwilling, it seems, I should know
    all her undecent conduct in this business. – Well then,
    I'll leave you together and hope when I am gone you'll
    agree; if not, you and I shan't agree, sir.

HORNER [*aside*] What means the fool? – If she and I agree,   80
    'tis no matter what you and I do.
    [*Whispers to* MRS PINCHWIFE, *who makes signs with
    her hand for him* (PINCHWIFE) *to be gone.*]

PINCHWIFE In the meantime, I'll fetch a parson and find out
    Sparkish and disabuse him. You would have me fetch
    a parson, would you not? Well then – now I think I am
    rid of her, and shall have no more trouble with her.   85
    Our sisters and daughters, like usurers' money, are
    safest when put out; but our wives, like their writings,
    never safe but in our closets under lock and key.
    [*Exit* MR PINCHWIFE.]
    [*Enter* BOY.]

BOY Sir Jaspar Fidget, sir, is coming up.
    [*Exit.*]

95 *The old style:* Horner indicates here that he is about to resume his pretence as the woman-hating 'eunuch'.

103 *masquerade:* See note on Act III, Scene I, line 103.

115 *anon:* soon, later

116 *private feast:* What do you feel is the effect of this metaphor in which sex is likened to eating? How typical is it of the language used by Horner and his fellow wits?

HORNER Here's the trouble of a cuckold, now, we are   90
    talking of. A pox on him! Has he not enough to do to
    hinder his wife's sport but he must other women's too?
    – Step in here, madam.
      [*Exit* MRS PINCHWIFE.]
      [*Enter* SIR JASPAR.]

SIR JASPAR My best and dearest friend.

HORNER [*aside to* QUACK] The old style, doctor. – Well,   95
    be short, for I am busy. What would your impertinent
    wife have now?

SIR JASPAR Well guessed, i'faith, for I do come from her.

HORNER To invite me to supper. Tell her I can't come; go.

SIR JASPAR Nay, now you are out, faith, for my lady and   100
    the whole knot of the virtuous gang, as they call
    themselves, are resolved upon a frolic of coming to you
    tonight in a masquerade and are all dressed already.

HORNER I shan't be at home.

SIR JASPAR [*aside*] Lord, how churlish he is to women! –   105
    Nay, prithee don't disappoint 'em; they'll think 'tis my
    fault. Prithee don't. I'll send in the banquet and the
    fiddles. But make no noise on't, for the poor virtuous
    rogues would not have it known for the world that
    they go a-masquerading, and they would come to no   110
    man's ball but yours.

HORNER Well, well – get you gone and tell 'em, if they
    come, 'twill be at the peril of their honour and yours.

SIR JASPAR Heh, he, he! – we'll trust you for that; farewell.
      [*Exit* SIR JASPAR.]

HORNER Doctor, anon you too shall be my guest,   115
    But now I'm going to a private feast.
      [*Exeunt.*]

Act V, Scene III

1 Stage direction *(with the letter in his hand):* This is the letter written by Margery as though from Alithea. Pinchwife has presented it to Sparkish.

5–6 *You are a frank person:* Pinchwife cannot resist the temptation to remind Sparkish of the adjective which he used about himself in Act III, Scene II – 'frank'.

23 *nay more, his verses on her:* even worse, had refused to listen to his love poetry

24 *torch:* flaming torch used to light the way

25 Stage direction *(Enter Alithea):* Alithea is quite ignorant of this most recent intrigue. How will she react to these developments? Lucy reminds the audience here, through her asides, of her leading role in the plotting to free Alithea from her engagement to Sparkish.

Act Five   Scene Three

[The scene changes to the Piazza of Covent Garden.]

[SPARKISH, PINCHWIFE.]

Sparkish *[with the letter in his hand]* But who would have
thought a woman could have been false to me? By the
world, I could not have thought it.

Pinchwife You were for giving and taking liberty; she has
taken it only, sir, now you find in that letter. You are a   5
frank person and so is she you see there.

Sparkish Nay, if this be her hand – for I never saw it.

Pinchwife 'Tis no matter whether that be her hand or no; I
am sure this hand, at her desire, led her to Mr Horner,
with whom I left her just now, to go fetch a parson to   10
'em, at their desire too, to deprive you of her forever,
for it seems yours was but a mock marriage.

Sparkish Indeed, she would needs have it that 'twas
Harcourt himself in a parson's habit that married us,
but I'm sure he told me 'twas his brother Ned.   15

Pinchwife Oh, there 'tis out, and you were deceived, not
she, for you are such a frank person – but I must be
gone. You'll find her at Mr Horner's; go and believe
your eyes.
    [Exit MR PINCHWIFE.]

Sparkish Nay, I'll to her and call her as many crocodiles,   20
sirens, harpies and other heathenish names as a poet
would do a mistress who had refused to hear his suit,
nay more, his verses on her. – But stay, is not that she
following a torch at t'other end of the Piazza? And
from Horner's certainly – 'tis so.   25
    [Enter ALITHEA, following a torch, and LUCY behind.]

219

35-40 What do you notice about Sparkish's language in denouncing Alithea during this scene?

35 *easy:* naive

40 *undo:* ruin

43 *merry:* drunk too much

52 *clubbed:* conspired

You are well met, madam, though you don't think so.
What, you have made a short visit to Mr Horner, but I
suppose you'll return to him presently; by that time the
parson can be with him.

ALITHEA Mr Horner, and the parson, sir!　　　　　　　　　　30

SPARKISH Come, madam, no more dissembling, no more
jilting, for I am no more a frank person.

ALITHEA How's this?

LUCY [*aside*] So, 'twill work, I see.

SPARKISH Could you find out no easy country fool to　　　　35
abuse? None but me, a gentleman of wit and pleasure
about the town? But it was your pride to be too hard
for a man of parts, unworthy false woman, false as a
friend that lends a man money to lose, false as dice
who undo those that trust all they have to 'em.　　　　　　40

LUCY [*aside*] He has been a great bubble by his similes, as
they say.

ALITHEA You have been too merry, sir, at your wedding
dinner, sure.

SPARKISH What, d'ye mock me too?　　　　　　　　　　　45

ALITHEA Or you have been deluded.

SPARKISH By you.

ALITHEA Let me understand you.

SPARKISH Have you the confidence – I should call it
something else, since you know your guilt – to stand　　　50
my just reproaches? You did not write an impudent
letter to Mr Horner, who I find now has clubbed with
you in deluding me with his aversion for women, that I
might not, forsooth, suspect him for my rival.

LUCY [*aside*] D'ye think the gentleman can be jealous　　　55
now, madam?

ALITHEA I write a letter to Mr Horner!

SPARKISH Nay, madam, do not deny it; your brother
showed it me just now and told me likewise he left you
at Horner's lodging to fetch a parson to marry you to　　　60

65–6 Alithea's only 'moral' attachment to Sparkish, his lack of jealousy, can now be broken.

76 *portion:* dowry

80 *cully:* foolish man

88–98 Alithea here accepts that she entered into her engagement with Sparkish on foolish grounds as an 'over-wise woman of the town'. She has learnt from her experience.

him, and I wish you joy, madam, joy, joy, and to him
too, much joy, and to myself more joy for not
marrying you.

ALITHEA [*aside*] So, I find my brother would break off the
match, and I can consent to't, since I see this   65
gentleman can be made jealous. – O Lucy, by his rude
usage and jealousy, he makes me almost afraid I am
married to him. Art thou sure 'twas Harcourt himself
and no parson that married us?

SPARKISH No, madam, I thank you. I suppose that was a   70
contrivance too of Mr Horner's and yours, to make
Harcourt play the parson; but I would as little as you
have him one now, no, not for the world, for shall I
tell you another truth? I never had any passion for you
till now, for now I hate you. 'Tis true I might have   75
married your portion, as other men of parts of the
town do sometimes, and so your servant, and to show
my unconcernedness, I'll come to your wedding and
resign you with as much joy as I would a stale wench
to a new cully, nay, with as much joy as I would after   80
the first night, if I had been married to you. There's for
you, and so your servant, servant.
    [*Exit* SPARKISH.]

ALITHEA How was I deceived in a man!

LUCY You'll believe, then, a fool may be made jealous
now? For that easiness in him that suffers him to be   85
led by a wife will likewise permit him to be persuaded
against her by others.

ALITHEA But marry Mr Horner! My brother does not
intend it, sure; if I thought he did, I would take thy
advice and Mr Harcourt for my husband. And now I   90
wish that if there be any over-wise woman of the town
who, like me, would marry a fool for fortune, liberty
or title; first, that her husband may love play and be a
cully to all the town but her and suffer none but

99–100 *may he not deserve it:* It would be a greater source of revengeful pleasure for a wronged wife to have a husband thought by others to be a cuckold, when, in fact, he is not – a very sophisticated idea for a maid!

fortune to be mistress of his purse; then, if for liberty,   95
that he may send her into the country under the
conduct of some housewifely mother-in-law, and, if for
title, may the world give 'em none but that of cuckold.

LUCY And for her greater curse, madam, may he not
deserve it.   100

ALITHEA Away, impertinent! – Is not this my old Lady
Lanterlu's?

LUCY Yes, madam. [*Aside*] And here I hope we shall find
Mr Harcourt.

    [*Exeunt* ALITHEA, LUCY.]

Act V, Scene IV

This is the final scene of the play. Before you read it, consider which elements of the plot remain to be resolved and what alternative outcomes there might be. For example, will Horner's 'secret' be revealed, or not? What would the implications be either way?

Enter Lady Fidget et al: The 'Ladies of honour' seem already a little the worse for drink. If you were directing the play, how would you signal this to the audience as they enter? Think about movement, posture and appearance as well as manner of speech.

2–3 *All I have now to do is to lock her in:*   In what sense is this line ironic?

16 *our women:*   our maids or servants

22 *brimmer:*   a full glass of wine

Act Five Scene Four

[*The scene changes again to* HORNER's *lodging.*]

[HORNER, LADY FIDGET, MRS DAINTY FIDGET, MRS
SQUEAMISH. *A table, banquet, and bottles.*]

HORNER [*aside*] A pox! They are come too soon – before I
    have sent back my new – mistress. All I have now to
    do is to lock her in, that they may not see her.

LADY FIDGET That we may be sure of our welcome, we have
    brought our entertainment with us and are resolved to   5
    treat thee, dear toad.

DAINTY And that we may be merry to purpose, have left
    Sir Jaspar and my old Lady Squeamish quarrelling at
    home at backgammon.

SQUEAMISH Therefore let us make use of our time, lest they   10
    should chance to interrupt us.

LADY FIDGET Let us sit then.

HORNER First, that you may be private, let me lock this
    door and that, and I'll wait upon you presently.

LADY FIDGET No, sir, shut 'em only and your lips forever,   15
    for we must trust you as much as our women.

HORNER You know all vanity's killed in me; I have no
    occasion for talking.

LADY FIDGET Now, ladies, supposing we had drank each of
    us our two bottles, let us speak the truth of our hearts.   20

DAINTY
                Agreed.
SQUEAMISH

LADY FIDGET By this brimmer, for truth is nowhere else to
    be found. [*Aside to* HORNER] Not in thy heart, false
    man!

29 *tyrants:* husbands

29–44 *Lady Fidget's song:* Do you feel that there is a serious point in Lady Fidget's words here?

40 *lick of the glass:* a drink from the glass

42 *red:* complexions

Horner [*aside to* LADY FIDGET] You have found me a   25
   true man, I'm sure.

Lady Fidget [*aside to* HORNER] Not every way. – But let
   us sit and be merry. [LADY FIDGET *sings*]

   1

   Why should our damned tyrants oblige us to live

   On the pittance of pleasure which they only give?   30

     We must not rejoice

     With wine and with noise.

   In vain we must wake in a dull bed alone,

   Whilst to our warm rival, the bottle, they're gone.

     Then lay aside charms   35

     And take up these arms.*

      The glasses.

   2

   'Tis wine only gives 'em their courage and wit;

   Because we live sober, to men we submit.

     If for beauties you'd pass,

     Take a lick of the glass;   40

   'Twill mend your complexions and, when they are gone,

   The best red we have is the red of the grape.

     Then, sisters, lay't on,

     And damn a good shape.

Dainty Dear brimmer! Well, in token of our openness and   45
   plain-dealing, let us throw our masks over our heads.

Horner So, 'twill come to the glasses anon.

Squeamish Lovely brimmer! Let me enjoy him first.

Lady Fidget No, I never part with a gallant till I've tried
   him. Dear brimmer, that mak'st our husbands   50
   shortsighted.

Dainty And our bashful gallants bold.

Squeamish And for want of a gallant, the butler lovely in
   our eyes. – Drink, eunuch.

Lady Fidget Drink, thou representative of a husband.   55
   Damn a husband!

59 Horner reminds the ladies, and the audience, of the supposed cause of his 'condition'.

62 *for the first:* refers to 'an English bawd' in line 59

64 *And the other's art:* refers to the French chirurgeon (surgeon) in line 59

66 *the vile distemper:* sexually transmitted disease

69 *stuffs:* materials for clothes, usually of high quality

72 *lie untumbled:* unsampled. Lady Fidget clearly intends a sexual pun as she develops the extended metaphor of women and clothing.

77 *druggets:* cheap, woollen material

82 *common house:* an ordinary restaurant or, by implication, a brothel

85 *sharp bent:* hungry

86 *ordinary:* simple restaurant or tavern

DAINTY And, as it were a husband, an old keeper.

SQUEAMISH And an old grandmother.

HORNER And an English bawd and a French chirurgeon.

LADY FIDGET Ay, we have all reason to curse 'em. 60

HORNER For my sake, ladies?

LADY FIDGET No, for our own, for the first spoils all young
gallants' industry.

DAINTY And the other's art makes 'em bold only with
common women. 65

SQUEAMISH And rather run the hazard of the vile distemper
amongst them than of a denial amongst us.

DAINTY The filthy toads choose mistresses now as they do
stuffs, for having been fancied and worn by others.

SQUEAMISH For being common and cheap. 70

LADY FIDGET Whilst women of quality, like the richest
stuffs, lie untumbled and unasked for.

HORNER Ay, neat and cheap and new often they think best.

DAINTY No, sir, the beasts will be known by a mistress
longer than by a suit. 75

SQUEAMISH And 'tis not for cheapness neither.

LADY FIDGET No, for the vain fops will take up druggets
and embroider 'em. But I wonder at the depraved
appetites of witty men; they use to be out of the
common road and hate imitation. Pray tell me, beast, 80
when you were a man, why you rather chose to club
with a multitude in a common house for an
entertainment than to be the only guest at a good table.

HORNER Why, faith, ceremony and expectation are
unsufferable to those that are sharp bent; people 85
always eat with the best stomach at an ordinary, where
every man is snatching for the best bit.

LADY FIDGET Though he get a cut over the fingers. – But I
have heard people eat most heartily of another man's
meat, that is, what they do not pay for. 90

93 *falling on briskly:* tucking in greedily. Again, there is a sense of sexual 'double entendre' here. See note on Act V, Scene II, line 116.

99 Read from the start of the scene, and then summarise the ladies' complaints up to this point.

106–147 In this section, the ladies' revelations are expressed non-realistically as a kind of chorus. How would you convey this aspect in performance? What is Horner's role during it? How do you think he should behave or react?

110 *Quaker:* religious group, properly known as the Society of Friends. They were often satirised in the seventeenth century for their supposed lack of integrity.

HORNER When they are sure of their welcome and
    freedom, for ceremony in love and eating is as
    ridiculous as in fighting; falling on briskly is all should
    be done in those occasions.

LADY FIDGET Well, then, let me tell you, sir, there is   95
    nowhere more freedom than in our houses and we take
    freedom from a young person as a sign of good
    breeding, and a person may be as free as he pleases
    with us, as frolic, as gamesome, as wild as he will.

HORNER Han't I heard you all declaim against wild men?   100

LADY FIDGET Yes, but for all that, we think wildness in a
    man as desirable a quality as in a duck or rabbit; a
    tame man, foh!

HORNER I know not, but your reputations frightened me,
    as much as your faces invited me.   105

LADY FIDGET Our reputation! Lord, why should you not
    think that we women make use of our reputation, as
    you men of yours, only to deceive the world with less
    suspicion? Our virtue is like the statesman's religion,
    the Quaker's word, the gamester's oath and the great   110
    man's honour – but to cheat those that trust us.

SQUEAMISH And that demureness, coyness and modesty
    that you see in our faces in the boxes at plays is as
    much a sign of a kind woman as a vizard-mask in the
    pit.   115

DAINTY For, I assure you, women are least masked when
    they have the velvet vizard on.

LADY FIDGET You would have found us modest women in
    our denials only.

SQUEAMISH Our bashfulness is only the reflection of the   120
    men's.

DAINTY We blush when they are shamefaced.

HORNER I beg your pardon, ladies; I was deceived in you
    devilishly. But why that mighty pretence to honour?

133 *honest:* chaste, faithful to their husbands

150 *receivers:* servants who accept bribes

151–2 *pass your grants:* accept your favours

154–7 *for your honour ... he takes up:* The meaning here is quite difficult. Horner's point is that for trusting ladies' honour to their gallants, he must in turn pawn his honour (financially) to the goldsmith/jeweller/china-seller who will demand payment punctually. So, in paying for the ladies' purchases at such places, he is, in effect, paying for them. It is a kind of indirect prostitution.

Lady Fidget We have told you. But sometimes 'twas for the   125
    same reason you men pretend business often, to avoid
    ill company, to enjoy the better and more privately
    those you love.

Horner But why would you ne'er give a friend a wink
    then?   130

Lady Fidget Faith, your reputation frightened us as much
    as ours did you, you were so notoriously lewd.

Horner And you so seemingly honest.

Lady Fidget Was that all that deterred you?

Horner And so expensive – you allow freedom, you say –   135

Lady Fidget Ay, ay.

Horner That I was afraid of losing my little money, as
    well as my little time, both which my other pleasures
    required.

Lady Fidget Money, foh! You talk like a little fellow now;   140
    do such as we expect money?

Horner I beg your pardon, madam; I must confess, I have
    heard that great ladies, like great merchants, set but
    the higher prices upon what they have, because they
    are not in necessity of taking the first offer.   145

Dainty Such as we make sale of our hearts?

Squeamish We bribed for our love? Foh!

Horner With your pardon, ladies, I know, like great men
    in offices, you seem to exact flattery and attendance
    only from your followers; but you have receivers about   150
    you and such fees to pay, a man is afraid to pass your
    grants. Besides, we must let you win at cards, or we
    lose your hearts, and if you make an assignation, 'tis at
    a goldsmith's, jeweller's or china house, where, for
    your honour you deposit to him, he must pawn his to   155
    the punctual cit, and so paying for what you take up,
    pays for what he takes up.

Dainty Would you not have us assured of our gallant's
    love?

164 *telling ripe:*   ready to be told. At this point, the discursive nature of the scene gives way to a series of revelations. It is soon clear that Horner has not revealed all to the audience.

189 *Harry Common:*   Harry Horner is shared with or common to them all.

191 *forsworn:*   found to have broken an oath

SQUEAMISH For love is better known by liberality than by   160
jealousy.

LADY FIDGET For one may be dissembled, the other not.
[*Aside*] But my jealousy can be no longer dissembled,
and they are telling ripe. – Come, here's to our gallants
in waiting, whom we must name, and I'll begin. This is   165
my false rogue. [*Claps him on the back*]

SQUEAMISH How!

HORNER So all will out now.

SQUEAMISH [*aside to* HORNER] Did you not tell me, 'twas
for my sake only you reported yourself no man?   170

DAINTY [*aside to* HORNER] Oh, wretch! Did you not
swear to me, 'twas for my love and honour you passed
for that thing you do?

HORNER So, so.

LADY FIDGET Come, speak, ladies; this is my false villain.   175

SQUEAMISH And mine too.

DAINTY And mine.

HORNER Well then, you are all three my false rogues too,
and there's an end on't.

LADY FIDGET Well then, there's no remedy; sister sharers, let   180
us not fall out, but have a care of our honour. Though
we get no presents, no jewels of him, we are savers of
our honour, the jewel of most value and use, which
shines yet to the world unsuspected, though it be
counterfeit.   185

HORNER Nay, and is e'en as good as if it were true,
provided the world think so, for honour, like beauty
now, only depends on the opinion of others.

LADY FIDGET Well, Harry Common, I hope you can be true
to three. Swear – but 'tis to no purpose to require your   190
oath, for you are as often forsworn as you swear to
new women.

HORNER Come, faith, madam, let us e'en pardon one
another, for all the difference I find betwixt we men

196 Stage direction *(Enter Sir Jaspar Fidget and Old Lady Squeamish):* The pace of the scene now changes as a series of brisk exits and entrances leading to the climax of the action ensues. The pivotal player in this is Horner himself in whose lodgings the scene is set.

and you women, we forswear ourselves at the   195
beginning of an amour, you as long as it lasts.
    [*Enter* SIR JASPAR FIDGET *and* OLD LADY
    SQUEAMISH.]

SIR JASPAR Oh, my Lady Fidget, was this your cunning, to
come to Mr Horner without me? But you have been
nowhere else, I hope.

LADY FIDGET No, Sir Jaspar.   200

OLD LADY SQUEAMISH And you came straight hither, Biddy?

SQUEAMISH Yes, indeed, Lady Grandmother.

SIR JASPAR 'Tis well, 'tis well; I knew when once they were
thoroughly acquainted with poor Horner, they'd ne'er
be from him. You may let her masquerade it with my   205
wife and Horner and I warrant her reputation safe.
    [*Enter* BOY.]

BOY Oh, sir, here's the gentleman come whom you bid
me not suffer to come up without giving you notice,
with a lady too, and other gentlemen –

HORNER Do you all go in there, whilst I send 'em away,   210
and, boy, do you desire 'em to stay below till I come,
which shall be immediately.
    [*Exeunt* SIR JASPAR, (OLD) LADY SQUEAMISH,
    LADY FIDGET, MRS DAINTY, SQUEAMISH.]

BOY Yes, sir.
    [*Exit.*]
    [*Exit* HORNER *at t'other door and returns with* MRS
    PINCHWIFE.]

HORNER You would not take my advice to be gone home
before your husband came back; he'll now discover all.   215
Yet pray, my dearest, be persuaded to go home and
leave the rest to my management. I'll let you down the
back way.

MRS PINCHWIFE I don't know the way home, so I don't.

HORNER My man shall wait upon you.   220

235 *mainly:* strongly

237 *a weak place:* insecure 'place' at Court

241 Pinchwife enters, speaking to Alithea.

242 *asseverations:* emphatic assertions

247–50 Horner's aside highlights his dilemma: How do you feel he will answer? Even at this relatively late stage in the play, new complications can occur.

MRS PINCHWIFE No, don't you believe that I'll go at all.
What, are you weary of me already?

HORNER No, my life, 'tis that I may love you long, 'tis to
secure my love, and your reputation with your
husband; he'll never receive you again else.   225

MRS PINCHWIFE What care I? D'ye think to frighten me with
that? I don't intend to go to him again; you shall be
my husband now.

HORNER I cannot be your husband, dearest, since you are
married to him.   230

MRS PINCHWIFE Oh, would you make me believe that?
Don't I see every day, at London here, women leave
their first husbands and go and live with other men as
their wives? Pish, pshaw, you'd make me angry, but
that I love you so mainly.   235

HORNER So, they are coming up – in again, in, I hear 'em.
    [*Exit* MRS PINCHWIFE.]
    Well, a silly mistress is like a weak place, soon got,
    soon lost, a man has scarce time for plunder; she
    betrays her husband first to her gallant and then her
    gallant to her husband.   240
    [*Enter* PINCHWIFE, ALITHEA, HARCOURT,
    SPARKISH, LUCY *and a Parson.*]

PINCHWIFE Come, madam, 'tis not the sudden change of
your dress, the confidence of your asseverations and
your false witness there, shall persuade me I did not
bring you hither just now; here's my witness, who
cannot deny it, since you must be confronted. – Mr   245
Horner, did not I bring this lady to you just now?

HORNER [*aside*] Now must I wrong one woman for
another's sake, but that's no new thing with me, for in
these cases I am still on the criminal's side, against the
innocent.   250

ALITHEA Pray, speak, sir.

253 The more outrageous the lie, the more likely Horner feels he is to be believed.

267–8 Do you approve of Horner's decision and justification for it? What are the likely consequences of his relationship with Harcourt?

HORNER [*aside*] It must be so – I must be impudent and try
  my luck; impudence uses to be too hard for truth.

PINCHWIFE What, you are studying an evasion or excuse for
  her. Speak, sir.   255

HORNER No, faith, I am something backward only to
  speak in women's affairs or disputes.

PINCHWIFE She bids you speak.

ALITHEA Ay, pray, sir, do; pray satisfy him.

HORNER Then truly, you did bring that lady to me just   260
  now.

PINCHWIFE O ho!

ALITHEA How, sir!

HARCOURT How, Horner!

ALITHEA What mean you, sir? I always took you for a man   265
  of honour.

HORNER [*aside*] Ay, so much a man of honour that I must
  save my mistress, I thank you, come what will on't.

SPARKISH So, if I had had her, she'd have made me believe
  the moon had been made of a Christmas pie.   270

LUCY [*aside*] Now could I speak, if I durst, and solve the
  riddle, who am the author of it.

ALITHEA O unfortunate woman! A combination against my
  honour, which most concerns me now, because you
  share in my disgrace, sir, and it is your censure, which   275
  I must now suffer, that troubles me, not theirs.

HARCOURT Madam, then have no trouble, you shall now
  see 'tis possible for me to love too, without being
  jealous; I will not only believe your innocence myself,
  but make all the world believe it. [*Apart to* HORNER]   280
  Horner, I must now be concerned for this lady's
  honour.

HORNER And I must be concerned for a lady's honour too.

HARCOURT This lady has her honour and I will protect it.

HORNER My lady has not her honour but has given it me   285
  to keep and I will preserve it.

289–90   Another very popular line always certain to produce a great laugh. What dramatic effect does the line have?

312   How is this line delivered?

changeling: a person believed to have been left at birth by the fairies

Harcourt I understand you not.

Horner I would not have you.

Mrs Pinchwife [*peeping in behind*] What's the matter with
'em all?   290

Pinchwife Come, come, Mr Horner, no more disputing.
Here's the parson; I brought him not in vain.

Harcourt No, sir, I'll employ him, if this lady please.

Pinchwife How! What d'ye mean?

Sparkish Ay, what does he mean?   295

Horner Why, I have resigned your sister to him; he has
my consent.

Pinchwife But he has not mine, sir; a woman's injured
honour, no more than a man's, can be repaired or
satisfied by any but him that first wronged it; and you   300
shall marry her presently, or –
      [*Lays his hand on his sword*]
      [*Enter to them* MRS PINCHWIFE.]

Mrs Pinchwife [*aside*] O Lord, they'll kill poor Mr Horner!
Besides, he shan't marry her whilst I stand by and look
on; I'll not lose my second husband so.

Pinchwife What do I see?   305

Alithea My sister in my clothes!

Sparkish Ha!

Mrs Pinchwife [*to* MR PINCHWIFE] Nay, pray now don't
quarrel about finding work for the parson; he shall
marry me to Mr Horner, for now, I believe, you have   310
enough of me.

Horner Damned, damned, loving changeling!

Mrs Pinchwife Pray, sister, pardon me for telling so many
lies of you.

Harcourt I suppose the riddle is plain now.   315

Lucy No, that must be my work. Good sir, hear me.
      [*Kneels to* MR PINCHWIFE, *who stands doggedly, with
      his hat over his eyes.*]

317–21 What style of drama do you think that Wycherley is parodying here?

324 *communicated:* had sex

334 *wheedle:* deceive

335–6 Sir Jaspar's self-satisfied smugness evaporates instantly.

340 *libidinous:* promiscuous

PINCHWIFE I will never hear woman again, but make 'em
   all silent, thus –
    [*Offers to draw upon his wife*]
HORNER No, that must not be.
PINCHWIFE You then shall go first; 'tis all one to me.   320
    [*Offers to draw on* HORNER; *stopped by* HARCOURT.]
HARCOURT Hold!
    [*Enter* SIR JASPAR FIDGET, LADY FIDGET, (OLD)
    LADY SQUEAMISH, MRS DAINTY FIDGET, MRS
    SQUEAMISH.]
SIR JASPAR What's the matter, what's the matter, pray,
   what's the matter, sir? I beseech you communicate, sir.
PINCHWIFE Why, my wife has communicated, sir, as your
   wife may have done too, sir, if she knows him, sir.   325
SIR JASPAR Pshaw, with him? Ha, ha, he!
PINCHWIFE D'ye mock me, sir? A cuckold is a kind of a
   wild beast; have a care, sir.
SIR JASPAR No, sure, you mock me, sir – he cuckold you! It
   can't be, ha, ha, he! Why, I tell you, sir –   330
    [*Offers to whisper*]
PINCHWIFE I tell you again, he has whored my wife, and
   yours too, if he knows her, and all the women he
   comes near; 'tis not his dissembling, his hypocrisy can
   wheedle me.
SIR JASPAR How! does he dissemble? Is he a hypocrite?   335
   Nay, then – how – wife – sister, is he an hypocrite?
OLD LADY SQUEAMISH An hypocrite, a dissembler! Speak,
   young harlotry, speak, how?
SIR JASPAR Nay, then – O, my head too! – O thou
   libidinous lady!   340
OLD LADY SQUEAMISH O thou harloting harlotry! Hast thou
   done't then?
SIR JASPAR Speak, good Horner, art thou a dissembler, a
   rogue? Hast thou –
HORNER Soh –   345

346–7 Lucy draws attention to the fact that Margery holds the key here. If she will keep quiet, ie lie, Horner's position can be maintained. But will she?

365 *say me nay:* deny my words

368 How should Horner deliver this line to gain a comic response from the audience?

372 *excuse:* explain

LUCY [*apart to* HORNER] I'll fetch you off, and her too, if she will but hold her tongue.

HORNER [*apart to* LUCY] Canst thou? I'll give thee –

LUCY [*to* MR PINCHWIFE] Pray have but patience to hear me, sir, who am the unfortunate cause of all this   350
confusion. Your wife is innocent, I only culpable, for I put her upon telling you all these lies concerning my mistress, in order to the breaking off the match between Mr Sparkish and her, to make way for Mr Harcourt.   355

SPARKISH Did you so, eternal rotten tooth? Then, it seems, my mistress was not false to me, I was only deceived by you. – Brother that should have been, now man of conduct, who is a frank person now? To bring your wife to her lover – ha!   360

LUCY I assure you, sir, she came not to Mr Horner out of love, for she loves him no more –

MRS PINCHWIFE Hold, I told lies for you, but you shall tell none for me, for I do love Mr Horner with all my soul, and nobody shall say me nay. Pray, don't you go to   365
make poor Mr Horner believe to the contrary; 'tis spitefully done of you, I'm sure.

HORNER [*aside to* MRS PINCHWIFE] Peace, dear idiot.

MRS PINCHWIFE Nay, I will not peace.

PINCHWIFE Not till I make you.   370

    [*Enter* DORILANT, QUACK.]

DORILANT Horner, your servant; I am the doctor's guest, he must excuse our intrusion.

QUACK But what's the matter, gentlemen? For heaven's sake, what's the matter?

HORNER Oh, 'tis well you are come. 'Tis a censorious   375
world we live in; you may have brought me a reprieve, or else I had died for a crime I never committed, and these innocent ladies had suffered with me. Therefore

390–91 Pinchwife is here referring to death caused by duelling which, though common, was illegal. Presumably, doctors were sometimes prepared to cover up such fatalities – for a price!

404 *capon:* a castrated cockerel, hence an impotent person

407 What do they do to silence Margery?

pray satisfy these worthy, honourable, jealous
gentlemen – that – [*Whispers*]   380

QUACK O, I understand you; is that all? [*Whispers to* SIR
JASPAR] Sir Jaspar, by heavens and upon the word of
a physician, sir –

SIR JASPAR Nay, I do believe you truly. – Pardon me, my
virtuous lady and dear of honour.   385

OLD LADY SQUEAMISH What, then all's right again?

SIR JASPAR Ay, ay, and now let us satisfy him too.
[*They whisper with* MR PINCHWIFE.]

PINCHWIFE An eunuch! Pray, no fooling with me.

QUACK I'll bring half the chirurgeons in town to swear it.

PINCHWIFE They! – they'll swear a man that bled to death   390
through his wounds died of an apoplexy.

QUACK Pray hear me, sir – why, all the town has heard the
report of him.

PINCHWIFE But does all the town believe it?

QUACK Pray inquire a little, and first of all these.   395

PINCHWIFE I'm sure when I left the town he was the lewdest
fellow in't.

QUACK I tell you, sir, he has been in France since; pray,
ask but these ladies and gentlemen, your friend Mr
Dorilant. – Gentlemen and ladies, han't you all heard   400
the late sad report of poor Mr Horner?

ALL THE LADIES Ay, ay, ay.

DORILANT Why, thou jealous fool, dost thou doubt it? He's
an arrant French capon.

MRS PINCHWIFE 'Tis false, sir, you shall not disparage poor   405
Mr Horner, for to my certain knowledge –

LUCY Oh, hold!

SQUEAMISH [*aside to* LUCY] Stop her mouth!

LADY FIDGET [*to* PINCHWIFE] Upon my honour, sir, 'tis as
true –   410

DAINTY D'ye think we would have been seen in his
company?

415 *secret to a fool:* This refers to Margery. What does it tell you about the morality of a play in which honesty is described as foolishness? Margery's honesty is, ironically, rather suspect.

423 *cast:* throw of the dice

426 *kept up:* restrained

429 *edify:* understand

437 *murrain:* cattle plague

SQUEAMISH Trust our unspotted reputations with him!

LADY FIDGET [*aside to* HORNER] This you get, and we too,
by trusting your secret to a fool.   415

HORNER Peace, madam. [*Aside to* QUACK] Well, doctor,
is not this a good design, that carries a man on
unsuspected and brings him off safe?

PINCHWIFE [*aside*] Well, if this were true, but my wife –
[DORILANT *whispers with* MRS PINCHWIFE.]

ALITHEA Come, brother, your wife is yet innocent, you see;   420
but have a care of too strong an imagination, lest like
an overconcerned, timorous gamester, by fancying an
unlucky cast, it should come. Women and fortune are
truest still to those that trust 'em.

LUCY And any wild thing grows but the more fierce and   425
hungry for being kept up and more dangerous to the
keeper.

ALITHEA There's doctrine for all husbands, Mr Harcourt.

HARCOURT I edify, madam, so much that I am impatient till
I am one.   430

DORILANT And I edify so much by example I will never be
one.

SPARKISH And because I will not disparage my parts I'll
ne'er be one.

HORNER And I, alas, can't be one.   435

PINCHWIFE But I must be one – against my will, to a
country wife, with a country murrain to me.

MRS PINCHWIFE [*aside*] And I must be a country wife still
too, I find, for I can't, like a city one, be rid of my
musty husband and do what I list.   440

HORNER Now, sir, I must pronounce your wife innocent,
though I blush whilst I do it, and I am the only man by
her now exposed to shame, which I will straight drown
in wine, as you shall your suspicion, and the ladies'
troubles we'll divert with a ballet. – Doctor, where are   445
your maskers?

448   *end of:*   aim in

451   *was it not, madam? Speak:*   What tone of voice should Lucy use here?

459   *puther:*   fuss, turmoil

   but court: only show-off

459–62   What is Horner's point in these final lines?

LUCY Indeed, she's innocent, sir, I am her witness; and her
end of coming out was but to see her sister's wedding
and what she has said to your face of her love to Mr
Horner was but the usual innocent revenge on a   450
husband's jealousy – was it not, madam? Speak.

MRS PINCHWIFE [*aside to* LUCY *and* HORNER] Since
you'll have me tell more lies – Yes, indeed, bud.

PINCHWIFE For my own sake fain I would all believe;
Cuckolds, like lovers, should themselves deceive.   455
But – [*Sighs*]
His honour is least safe, too late I find,
Who trusts it with a foolish wife or friend.
    [*A dance of cuckolds.*]

HORNER Vain fops but court and dress and keep a puther,
To pass for women's men with one another,   460
But he who aims by women to be priz'd,
First by the men, you see, must be despis'd.

255

Epilogue

Spoken by Mrs Knepp – she was the actress who first played the role of Lady Fidget.

1 *vigorous:* lively men (ironic)

15 *buckram:* stiff, but also, when linked to the reference to William Shakespeare's Falstaff, in *Henry IV* and *V*, probably meaning illusory

18 *essenced:* perfumed

22 *Flanders mares:* Flemish (from northern Belgium) horses were imported mainly for breeding which makes the satirical point stronger.

33 *cozening:* cheating

What do you think that the main point of the Epilogue is and why has Lady Fidget been chosen to deliver it?

EPILOGUE,
spoken by MRS KNEPP

Now, you the vigorous, who daily here
O'er vizard-mask in public domineer,
And what you'd do to her if in place where,
Nay, have the confidence to cry, 'Come out',
Yet when she says 'Lead on', you are not stout,   5
But to your well-dressed brother straight turn round
And cry, 'Pox on her, Ned, she can't be sound',
Then slink away, a fresh one to engage,
With so much seeming heat and loving rage,
You'd frighten listening actress on the stage,   10
Till she at last has seen you huffing come
And talk of keeping in the tiring-room,
Yet cannot be provok'd to lead her home.
Next, you Falstaffs of fifty, who beset
Your buckram maidenheads, which your friends get,   15
And whilst to them you of achievements boast,
They share the booty and laugh at your cost.
In fine, you essenced boys, both old and young,
Who would be thought so eager, brisk and strong,
Yet do the ladies, not their husbands, wrong,   20
Whose purses for your manhood make excuse,
And keep your Flanders mares for show, not use:
Encourag'd by our woman's man today,
A Horner's part may vainly think to play
And may intrigues so bashfully disown   25
That they may doubted be by few or none,
May kiss the cards at picquet, ombre, loo,
And so be thought to kiss the lady too;
But, gallants, have a care, faith, what you do.
The world, which to no man his due will give,   30
You by experience know you can deceive
And men may still believe you vigorous,
But then we women – there's no cozening us.

257

RESOURCE NOTES

Who has written *The Country Wife* and why?

Who was William Wycherley?

William Wycherley, the eldest son of a country gentleman, was born in 1640, near Shrewsbury. He was educated at home by his intelligent but rather stern and imposing father before being sent to France at the age of 15 to continue his studies. Whilst there, he became a Catholic and returned to England in 1660, the year in which Charles II became monarch. He took up a place at Queen's College, Oxford, but as his temperament was clearly unsuited to university life, he lasted less than a year before commencing legal studies at the Inner Temple in London.

In the capital, Wycherley found his cultural and spiritual home. As a young student, he began to experience and greatly enjoy the life of a fashionable and carefree 'man about town'. He was turning into just the sort of 'wit' he was later to present so successfully on stage. At about this time, too, he began his career writing poetry and eventually his first play, *Love in a Wood*, produced in 1671. This was an immediate success, a fact which established him socially as well as artistically. He became a favourite amongst the court circle and he enjoyed a well-publicised affair with a courtier, Barbara Palmer, later to become mother of three of the king's sons. Another former member of the court circle, Major Pack, noted in his memoirs in 1728:

> As King Charles was extremely fond of him [Wycherley] upon
> account of his Wit, some of the royal mistresses set no less
> value upon Those Parts in him, of which they were more proper
> judges.

Wycherley's writing career was dazzling but brief. He wrote only three more plays, *The Gentleman Dancing Master* (1672), *The Country Wife* and *The Plain Dealer* (both 1676). With his reputation at its height, Wycherley fell dangerously ill. He was visited in person by the king, who financed a recuperative holiday to France, where he stayed until 1679. By the time of his return, his creative gifts had forsaken him and he took employment as personal tutor to one of the king's illegitimate sons. The king's patronage was relatively short-lived, however, as he disapproved of the fact that Wycherley had secretly married the widow of the Earl of Drogheda. Mrs Inchbald, a former actress, writing in 1706, observes a particular irony in Wycherley's declining fortunes:

> As the catastrophe of all comedies is marriage, marriage was
> likewise the catastrophe of all poor Wycherley's own schemes;
> for he married, and the rest of his life was a deep tragedy.

Although this may be an over-simplification of events, happiness and stability in Wycherley's life were elusive. Legal disputes over his dead wife's estate led him to imprisonment for debt, and even after his release he was in severe financial straits and his health also deteriorated.

In 1697, Wycherley inherited his father's estate and was able to return to London after an extensive period of enforced absence. For over fifteen years he became something of a literary legend, advising a new generation of writers such as the poet Alexander Pope. He died in 1715, and was buried in St Paul's Church, Covent Garden. Although to modern audiences and readers he may seem a rather obscure literary figure, it is worth noting that Wycherley's critical reputation in the early eighteenth century was very high indeed. Lord Lansdowne, writing in 1718, remarked:

> When he [Wycherley] had published some of his plays and
> other things of a Poetick Nature, he was universally admired
> and reckoned in the first rank of Comic Poets and the next
> excellent to Ben Jonson.

✦ *Activity*

Eighteenth-century writers were very fond of recording or celebrating the lives of the famous in poetry. On your own, or in pairs, write a verse tribute to the life of William Wycherley using some of the information above and your knowledge of *The Country Wife*. You might choose to use the form which Wycherley himself uses for his Prologue and Epilogue in *The Country Wife*. Note how the verse is written primarily in ten-syllable rhyming couplets. You may also wish to imitate the style of language used in the seventeenth and eighteenth centuries (an approach known as *pastiche*).

Political and theatrical background of the Restoration

Officially, English drama came to an end in 1642 for eighteen years, until the Restoration of Charles II in 1660. During this time, known as the Interregnum (interruption of the monarchy), Civil War prevailed, followed by a lengthy period of Puritan government. Parliament banned all plays as immoral, and the theatres were closed, although illicit performances of various sorts undoubtedly took place. These were constantly under threat of being raided by authorities who recognised the power of drama to influence, as well as to entertain, the public.

The euphoria that greeted Charles's return to London on 29 May 1660, set the social, cultural and political tone for his reign, and its peculiar energy and self-confidence is expressed, perhaps, best of all in the astonishing developments in the theatre. 'Restoration drama' actually includes a greater variety of work than the dozen or so frequently revived plays from the period (including *The Country Wife*). Heroic tragedies in which comic-style supermen grappled with decisions about love and honour in far-flung exotic places were extremely popular, although to modern audiences they would probably seem absurdly melodramatic. These were generally written in verse and were heavily influenced by French writers such as Pierre Corneille (1606–1684), just as the writers of comedies, including Wycherley in *The Country Wife*, were to be influenced by the French contemporary playwright of genius, Molière (1622–1673).

Comedy was very much, then, the spirit of the age, although it is impossible to define the typical Restoration comedy. The literary period known as the Restoration (as opposed to the twenty-five years of Charles II's reign) covers nearly half a century and includes great changes in styles of theatres and styles of acting. It is also salutary to note that the plays which are considered to be masterpieces of the time, *The Country Wife*, William Congreve's *The Way of the World* (1700) or John Vanbrugh's *The Relapse* (1697), were not the greatest popular successes. Nevertheless, the most important common element in Restoration comedies is their authors' interest in contemporary social customs, conventions and relationships, almost invariably with a realistic London setting.

Theatres

Most of the theatres which had been in existence before the Civil War had been demolished or had become obsolete. In addition, it had not been the custom for the Court, the most important patrons of the theatrical revolution, to visit public playhouses at all: this was a habit which Charles II had learned to enjoy during his time in France and wanted to continue at home.

In order to accommodate royal visits, a new kind of theatre had to evolve, and since building from scratch was expensive, the first new theatres were converted Royal or 'Real' tennis courts. They gave the basic auditorium shape, including the proscenium arch and stage in the style of a picture frame, which became the convention in theatres for over 300 years. After these first theatres came two new purpose-built theatres in and around Covent Garden and Drury Lane, and thus the area of London now known as 'the West End' was born. These theatres were the only ones permitted to open and were wholly controlled by the Court, catering almost exclusively for aristocratic tastes and audiences. Wycherley and his contemporaries had little choice but to give the audience what they appeared to want – a reflection of themselves and their lifestyle – and *The Country Wife* is no exception to this.

Styles of acting

A Prologue to William Shakespeare's play *Othello*, performed in 1660, contained the following lines:

> I come, unknown to any of the rest
> To tell you news, I saw the lady drest
> The Woman plays today, mistake me not,
> No Man in gown, or page in petty-coat ...

With these words, a woman called Margaret Hughes was led forward by a male colleague on to the stage to perform the role of Desdemona in the play. He went on:

> ... and how d'ye like her, come what is it ye drive at?
> She's the same thing in public as in private;
> As far from being what you call a Whore
> As Desdemona innur'd by the Moor?

Margaret Hughes was the first actress ever to appear on the London stage, a direct consequence of Charles II's insistence that only women should play female roles. This was a momentous decision both for the way in which already existing female roles could be played, and for the influence it had on plays to be written in the future.

Possibly the most famous actress of the Restoration period was Charles II's mistress, Nell Gwynn, although her artistic talents are a matter of some debate. It has been said that to describe her as an actress is to do the profession an injustice, while others claim she was a witty and gifted comedienne. Samuel Pepys, a celebrated diarist of the period and a keen theatre-goer, considered her in general to be a dreadful performer, but in this extract from his diary, he is rather more complimentary:

> 22 March 1667. After dinner with my wife to the King's House to see *The Maiden Queen*, a new play of Dryden's ... and the truth is that there is a comical part done by Nell ... that I can never hope to see the like of again, done by man or woman. But so great a performance of a comical part was never, I believe in

the world before as Nell does this, both as a mad girl, then
most and best of all when she comes in like a young gallant;
and hath the motions and carriage of a spark the most that I
saw any man have. It makes me, I confess, admire her.

(*Diary of Samuel Pepys*)

✦ *Activities*

1 Use the time-line on pages 264–265 as a starting point to
prepare a class/group collage on the Restoration period.
Further research could include:

- art, music and architecture (including landscape gardening);
- social development, especially the differences between
town and country;
- political developments in Europe.

2a How do you think that the arrival of actresses affected the
ways in which existing female roles were performed? How
did they affect the development of new plays?

b It is as hard a matter for a pretty Woman to keep herself honest
in a Theatre, as 'tis for an Apothecary to keep his Treacle from
the flies in hot Weather.

(Thomas Brown, 1720, quoted in Robert C. Lawrence,
Introduction to Restoration Plays)

What does this remark indicate to you about society's
attitude both to women and to the theatre in 1720?

c Imagine that Samuel Pepys had been present at Margaret
Hughes' revolutionary appearance as the first actress in
England. Write his diary entry for that evening, describing
what he saw and putting forward his own views on the
subject. Look again at Pepys' comment on Nell Gwynn
above to get some idea of his style.

✦

Dates	Theatrical events	Historical and literary events
1642	Theatres closed by Act of Parliament	Outbreak of Civil War; Charles I leaves London
1649		Execution of Charles I
1658		Oliver Cromwell dies
1660	Introduction of actresses on stage	Charles II crowned. The Restoration period begins
1666		Great Fire of London
1667		*Paradise Lost* published by John Milton
1671	*The Rehearsal* – George Villiers, Duke of Buckingham	Milton's *Paradise Regained* and *Samson Agonistes* published
1672	Playwrights Joseph Addison and Richard Steele born. *Marriage à la Mode* – John Dryden	
1674	King's Company opens Drury Lane Theatre	Milton dies
1675	*The Country Wife* – William Wycherley	
1676	*The Man of Mode* – George Etherege. *The Plain Dealer* – Wycherley	
1677	*All For Love* - Dryden	
1685	Theatres closed for three months	Death of Charles II. Accession of James II
1688		Flight of James II after defeat in 'Glorious Revolution'

1689		Accession of William and Mary
1691	George Etherege dies	
1693	*The Old Bachelor* and *The Double Dealer* – William Congreve	
1694	Theatres closed for Queen Mary's death	Death of Queen Mary
1695	*Love for Love* – Congreve	
1696	*Love's Last Shift* – Colly Cibber. *The Relapse* – John Vanbrugh. Lord Chamberlain requires all plays licensed	
1698	Jeremy Collier publishes *A Short View of the Immorality and Profaneness of the English Stage*	
1700	*The Way of the World* – Congreve. *The Constant Couple* – George Farquhar	Dryden dies
1702		Death of William III. Accession of Queen Anne
1706	*The Recruiting Officer* – Farquhar	
1707	*The Beaux' Stratagem* – Farquhar. George Farquhar dies	Playwright and novelist, Henry Fielding born. Union of England and Scotland
1709		Samuel Johnson born
1714		Death of Queen Anne. Accession of George I

What type of text is *The Country Wife*?

The most straightforward way to define *The Country Wife* is that it is a comedy written during the historical/literary period known as the Restoration. Although the term 'Restoration comedy' implies a distinct theatrical style, it is an over-simplified label since it tries to include literally hundreds of plays written over a period of more than 40 years.

What does the term 'comedy' mean?

If you study a Shakespeare play such as *Twelfth Night* or *As You Like It*, you will see that the word 'comedy' can embrace a number of features, not all of which are to do with humour.

✦ *Activity*

Look at the list of comic elements below, which are in no particular order of importance. For each, try to find at least one example from *The Country Wife*:

* complicated plans/intrigues which end in near disaster;
* successions of rapid entrances and exits (as in farce);
* double-meanings/puns/innuendoes, often of a sexual nature;
* slapstick;
* use of disguise;
* mistaken identity;
* fools/hypocrites who are exposed or ridiculed;
* verbal virtuosity or repartee, such as when clever or 'witty' remarks are made;
* exaggerated or idiosyncratic manners of speech;
* the good are 'rewarded' – the wicked are 'punished';
* use of dramatic/situational irony (the audience is more aware of what is going on than the characters);
* topical jokes about contemporary society (as in pantomime);
* characters who emerge from their experiences as wiser and 'better' people;
* a happy ending.

a Are there any features which you could not find examples of in *The Country Wife*?

b Which of the above do you feel are most applicable to and important in *The Country Wife*?

c Do you feel that there are any other comic ingredients in *The Country Wife* which are not listed above?

Comedy of manners?

The Country Wife is a play much concerned with the way in which people are expected to behave in social situations. Since this is a hallmark of many of the plays of the period, the term 'comedy of manners' has evolved to describe such dramatic work. Courtly Restoration society was itself obsessive about surface appearances, fashion and etiquette. The way of wearing one's wig and one's clothes and of holding one's fan carried subtle differences in meaning which a Restoration audience was acutely sensitive to, particularly when so physically close to the players on stage.

In performance, such details of conduct would have been lavishly and painstakingly emphasised, creating a highly artificial, polished style in which language and gesture were calculated to achieve the greatest effect on others. This style is sometimes described as 'mannered'.

Such an emphasis in drama on external features of social interaction inevitably produced a simplified notion of character. Individuality in characterisation tended to be less important than broadly recognisable social types which proliferate in the comedies of the Restoration. Most of these can be seen in *The Country Wife*:

- the gallants (or wits) – Horner, Harcourt, Dorilant;
- the fop – Sparkish;
- the cuckold – Sir Jaspar, Pinchwife;
- the women of 'honour' – Lady Fidget, Mrs Squeamish;
- the female 'wit' – Alithea and, eventually, Margery, Lucy;
- the country simpleton – Margery (to begin with).

✦ Activity

Below is a list of characters from various Restoration comedies. What social type from the list above do you think each is?

- Lady Wishfort (Wish-for-it), *The Way of the World*
- Sir Novelty Fashion, *Love's Last Shift*
- Sir Tunbelly, *The Relapse*
- Courtall, *She Would if She Could*
- Sir Fopling Flutter, *The Man of Mode*
- Manly, *The Plain Dealer*
- Berinthia, *The Relapse*
- Lady Fancyfull, *The Provoked Wife*
- Squire Sullen, *The Beaux Stratagem*

In later times, the tradition of the comedy of manners can be seen in eighteenth-century comedies such as Richard Brinsley Sheridan's *The School for Scandal* (1777) and Oliver Goldsmith's *She Stoops to Conquer* (1773). Examples in the nineteenth and twentieth centuries include Oscar Wilde's *The Importance of Being Earnest* (1895) and Noel Coward's *Hay Fever* (1924). More recent examples would be such television series as *Keeping Up Appearances* and *Absolutely Fabulous*.

Comedy of realism?

Many of the prologues and epilogues of Restoration comedies make the claim that the plays offered a realistic picture of life as it was, as in John Vanbrugh's *The Provoked Wife*:

> 'Tis the intent and business of the stage,
> To copy out the follies of the age,
> To hold to every man a faithful glass,
> And show him of what species he's an ass.

However, such a claim is hard to uphold when one considers the requirements of comic plotting, which involve complications well beyond what one would normally expect to encounter and, indeed, many of the comedies are resolved in a way which would have been a legal impossibility. Nevertheless, compared with comedy's counterpart, heroic tragedy, the world depicted was more familiar. Prose dialogue, too, though highly stylised and certainly no mere transcription of everyday speech, was far more realistic than tragedy with its heightened, poetic language.

More importantly, the stage conventions of the time undercut any deep sense of realism. Prologues and epilogues where characters address the audience directly, together with the aside, one of Restoration comedy's most distinctive devices, serve to remind the audience that art and life are quite different.

✦ Activity

Choose one scene or section of a scene from *The Country Wife* in which you feel the device of the aside has made a particularly strong contribution to the dramatic effect. Explain, in as much detail as you can, how the aside has helped:

- characterisation
- development of the plot/situation
- the creation of comedy
- any other effects you can detect.

Social satire?

Satire in literature aimed to hold up common follies and vices to public ridicule in order to reform some of the human weaknesses at work in society. Wycherley is often considered to be the most satirical of the Restoration playwrights, but it is still debatable how far he is criticising the excesses he depicts, and how far he is offering his portrayal of immorality for the sake of entertainment and amusement. Far from being satirical in nature (which implies a moral standpoint), *The Country Wife* has been accused of promoting immorality through the glamorous presentation of the rake Horner, and Wycherley's implied approval of Margery's adultery with him. (These issues are discussed further in 'How does *The Country Wife* present its subject?' on page 277.) Other outstanding examples of satire include:

- Jonathan Swift's eighteenth-century essay, *A Modest Proposal* (1729);
- the early novels of Evelyn Waugh, such as *Decline and Fall* (1928) and *Vile Bodies* (1930);
- the plays of Joe Orton, especially *Loot* (1966) and *What the Butler Saw* (1969);
- and, more recently, the British TV series *Not the Nine O'Clock News* and *Drop the Dead Donkey*.

✦ Activity

What do you feel are Wycherley's satirical targets in *The Country Wife*? Copy and complete the chart below (one example has been done for you). This should help you to focus on possible areas of satire more precisely.

Satirical target	Method of presentation	Evidence
Personal vanity and lack of self-awareness of the fop	The ironic characterisation of Sparkish, who is convinced that he is a true wit, when his words and behaviour show him to be a tedious bore	His first appearance in the play when he makes a long-winded feeble joke about Horner being 'a sign of a man'(Act I, Scene I, lines 307–347)

Poetic prose drama?

Although almost all of *The Country Wife* is written in prose, it has such remarkably sensuous, vivid and varied language that it might justifiably be described as 'poetic'.

✦ *Activity*

a One common feature of poetic prose is imagery. Skim and scan the text looking for as many examples as you can of imagery relating to:

- animals
- disease
- money/property
- sex
- violence.

b Can you detect any other patterns of images?

How was *The Country Wife* produced?

From page to stage

The Country Wife was first performed in January 1675, and published as a play text later in the same year. It was revived as part of the repertory of the Theatre Royal, Drury Lane in 1676, and was clearly popular enough to have been consistently revived well into the eighteenth century. By 1766, a new version called *The Country Girl* had been rewritten by the celebrated actor-manager, David Garrick, in which much of the original material, including the character of Horner, had been severely modified. Garrick's version was the only version which survived until the first modern production of the play in 1924.

Very little is known about how Wycherley came to write the play. It is generally assumed that he was strongly influenced by Molière's plays *L'École des Maris* (1661) and *L'École des Femmes* (1662), from which he borrowed devices such as the mistaken delivery of a letter and the use of disguise by a woman to escape imprisonment by her husband. The other well-known source is the play *Eunuchus* by the Latin poet Terence (c190–159 BC), in which the central character disguises himself as a eunuch to gain access to his lover.

What is fairly clear is that writing for the stage during the Restoration period would have been considered a practical rather than an artistic pastime. The demand for new plays at the two licensed playhouses was intense, and despite the lukewarm response to Wycherley's previous play, *The Gentleman Dancing Master* (see Prologue), he was in considerable demand. Furthermore, such was the nature of Restoration audiences that playwrights were very much in the business of giving the public what it wanted, and what it wanted, above all else, was a humorous reflection of itself.

Playhouses, audiences and players

Much has been written about those who regularly attended the playhouses during the Restoration, and it seems clear that there has probably never been a more homogeneous or privileged audience in theatre history. This was an audience which was exclusively urban, comfortably well-off (to afford the comparatively expensive ticket prices) and able and willing to attend on a regular basis. For them, theatre-going was not an occasional luxury but a regular form of recreation. As the critic J. L. Styan puts it:

> ... the playhouses were on a pleasure circuit which included the parks and the brothels, the gaming houses and the bagnios.
> (*Restoration Comedy in Performance*, 1986)

There is also considerable evidence that the audiences were extraordinarily badly behaved, often competing with the players for attention. For the fashionable wits, such as Sparkish, to be seen at a play was of equal importance to watching the performance:

> What then? It may be I have a pleasure in't [showing off his wife], as I have to show fine clothes at a playhouse the first day ...
> (Act III, Scene II, lines 391–393)

Like many other comedies of the period, *The Country Wife* is full of references to play-going, and indeed to the other 'pleasures of the town' which would have been enjoyed by the audiences – playing cards, dining and most of all, conducting secret assignations with current and future sexual partners. Wycherley, like his contemporaries, gives his plays a sense of realism by mentioning familiar places, sometimes 'within a stone's throw' of the theatre itself, for example Sparkish's lines:

> Come, but where do we dine? ... At Chateline's? ... Or at the Cock? ... Or at the Dog and Partridge?
> (Act I, Scene I, lines 370–376)

The sum effect, though, of such specific details of everyday life is, paradoxically, non-realistic. Audiences could never really forget that what they were watching on stage was not reality but a distorted form of it, and this perhaps explains the absurdly complicated and fairly unoriginal plotting and characterisation of Restoration comedies and the extensive use of such non-realistic devices as prologues and asides. The relative unimportance of plausibility was articulated by one of the finest Restoration playwrights, George Farquhar in 1699:

> The poet no more expects that you should believe the plot of the play than old Aesop desired the world should think his eagle and lion talked like you and I.
> (Quoted in J. L. Styan, *Restoration Comedy in Performance*)

By modern standards, there were relatively few players, and they would have been well known to the audiences; many plays would certainly have been written with particular actors in mind. Charles Hart, the original Horner, for example, was by all accounts a stunning-looking leading man and lived an off-stage life not too far removed from that of the character he played, numbering among his mistresses the king's favourite, Nell Gwynn.

The shape of the newly modified and redesigned 'tennis court' playhouses similarly discouraged a sense of realism. The actors performed on a thrust stage surrounded on three sides by the audience. There were no special lighting effects to heighten illusion, and audience and players shared the 'space' of the auditorium and the experience of performance. As the Restoration drew to a close, the auditoriums increased in size enormously, reducing the intimacy between players and audience and heralding a more realistic style of theatre.

✦ *Activities*

1 A familiar criticism of Restoration comedy is that the plots are too contrived. Construct a detailed scene-by-scene flow-chart of the plot of *The Country Wife*. For each scene, work out what you feel Wycherley's dramatic purpose is, then identify which scenes you feel are:

- particularly important for the development of the plot;
- of limited importance for the development of the plot.

What do you feel are the strengths and weaknesses of the plot of *The Country Wife* as a whole?

2 A particular headache for a director is how to stage-manage the final scene in which, according to the usual convention, all the characters need to appear on stage together. Using the diagram below, which is based on a design of a Restoration theatre, plot how you would 'block' (position) the characters to achieve the most satisfying effect, in your opinion. You need to take into account artistic/dramatic factors, such as ensuring the characters who are most important to the action are given 'centre stage', and practical factors, such as where actors can stand so that they can be seen by the audience and

SCENERY

B A L C O N I E S	Stage door		Stage door	B A L C O N I E S
	Stage door	APRON STAGE	Stage door	

PIT (audience)

not be 'masked'. Note that the balconies could also be used as part of the set.

Write a brief account of your plan, justifying the decisions which you have taken.

3 Choose one scene (or a part of a scene) from *The Country Wife* which you feel would have particular appeal for a modern audience. Imagine that you, as director of a production of the play, have to brief your cast on how you feel the scene should be played to bring out its full dramatic potential. Write the notes which you would give the cast to help them prepare for the scene. Some areas that you might consider are:

- interpretation of character
- interaction of characters
- movements/gestures/use of space
- timing and pacing of the scene
- how to achieve and sustain comedy.

How does *The Country Wife* present its subject?

The presentation of Horner

Horner is, with little doubt, the central character of *The Country Wife*, since his elaborate plan provides the mainspring and sustaining principle of the play's action. But how appropriate is the term 'hero' in his case?

✦ *Activities*

1 Write down a list of words which you associate with the term 'hero', and its derivatives 'heroic' and 'heroism'. Then compile a complementary list in which you write down words which you would use to describe Horner's behaviour and attitudes in the play. Compare your two lists.

2 In Act IV, Scene III, Horner famously describes himself as a 'Machiavel in love'. This implies that he is in complete control of the events which he has set in motion.

a Are there any moments in the play when you feel that Horner is not in control of events?

b Consider the following remark made about Horner by a modern theatre critic:

> Horner's heroic endeavours are inseparable from his almost horrifying single-mindedness. Similarly, the means by which he becomes the vehicle of Wycherley's satire of society's gullibility and hypocrisy is also, by its extraordinary thoroughness of motive and method, how Wycherley suggests that Horner has become his own victim.
> (John Dixon Hunt, Introduction to New Mermaid edition of *The Country Wife*)

How far would you agree that Horner is a victim? What evidence would you use to support this view?

The presentation of marriage

The audience is offered three principal marital situations to contemplate in *The Country Wife*:

- Pinchwife and Margery
- Sir Jaspar and Lady Fidget
- the proposed match between Alithea and Sparkish.

✦ *Activities*

If you are able to work in a group, assign each of the six characters above to a different individual. The task is to prepare for a 'hot-seating' exercise, in which the individual character in role is asked a series of questions by other members of the group. Alternatively, each character might present a brief monologue entitled 'My views on marriage'. It is important that the roleplays/monologues are prepared very thoroughly by careful research of the text. You might like to consider the following areas, finding as many specific examples as you can:

- the reason for the marriage (if known);
- what each character explicitly *says* about marriage, specifically or generally, in the play;
- what you deduce about the characters' attitudes to marriage by their *behaviour* in the play;
- the number of occasions when love and marriage are discussed in the context of *money*.

Having considered all the evidence, what view of marriage as a whole do you feel is being presented in the play?

Some further issues on these characters to discuss or reflect upon:

1a What similarities and differences do you find in the portrayal of the three fop/cuckold characters: Sparkish, Pinchwife and Sir Jaspar?

  b What does the apparent obsession with cuckoldry in *The Country Wife* indicate to you about:

- the relationship between the sexes in general, especially men's attitudes to women?

- the moral framework of the society presented by Wycherley?

c Sparkish is both a fop and a potential cuckold. What do you think that these two roles have in common?

2 What do you feel is Lady Fidget's role in the play?

3 Alithea is no simple heroine and those critics who see her and Harcourt as the standard by which Wycherley intends the other marriages to be judged miss much in her character.
(Gamini Salgado: *English Drama: A Critical Introduction*)

What do you make of this view of Alithea?

4a Margery is arguably the only character in the play who really develops. Consider in what ways she changes and whether, in your opinion, it is for the better or not.

b 'Through Margery, we learn just as much about the ways of the town as of the country.' How far do you agree with this statement?

5 To a large extent, the main characters of *The Country Wife* are differentiated and vitalised by their modes of speech. Select one speech of reasonable length by each of the main characters in the play which you feel is typical of that character, and identify what you think are the distinctive features of the speech.

As an alternative activity, imagine that each character writes a diary entry, describing what happens in the final scene of the play (when all the characters are present). The style of the entry should reflect the distinctive 'voice' of the writer.

The presentation of honour

The word 'honour', and words of similar meaning (synonyms) such as 'reputation', occur frequently throughout the play.

Below is a selective list of references to honour in the order in which they are said:

1 '... a good name is seldom got by giving it oneself, and women no more than honour are compassed by bragging.' (Act I, Scene I, lines 50–52)

2 'How, you saucy fellow! Would you wrong my honour?' (Act I, Scene I, lines 113–114)

3 ' ... your women of honour, as you call 'em, are only chary of their reputations, not their persons ...' (Act I, Scene I, lines 182–184)

4 ' ... the honour of your family shall sooner suffer in your wife there than in me ...' (Act II, Scene I, lines 47–49)

5 'I do assure you, he is ... a man of such perfect honour, he would say nothing to a lady he does not mean ...' (Act II, Scene I, lines 170–173)

6 'How! Did he disparage my parts? Nay, then my honour's concerned; I can't put up that, sir, by the world!' (Act II, Scene I, lines 309–311)

7 'Ay, my dear, dear of honour, thou hast still so much honour in thy mouth –
That she has none elsewhere' (Act II, Scene I, lines 437–439)

8 'Why, these are pretenders to honour, as critics to wit, only by censuring others; ...' (Act II, Scene I, lines 464–465)

9 'But I have so strong a faith in your honour, dear, dear, noble sir, that I'd forfeit mine for yours at any time, dear sir.' (Act II, Scene I, lines 607–609)

10 'But why, dearest madam, will you be more concerned for his honour than he is himself? Let his honour alone, for my sake and his. He, he has no honour ... But what my dear friend can guard himself.' (Act III, Scene II, lines 242–247)

11 'But what a devil is this honour! 'Tis sure a disease in the head, like the megrim, or falling sickness, that always hurries people away to do themselves mischief. Men lose their lives by it; women what's dearer to 'em, their love ...' (Act IV, Scene I, lines 32–36)

12 '... a woman's injured honour, no more than a man's, can be repaired or satisfied by any but him that first wronged it ... (*Lays his hand on his sword*)' (Act V, Scene IV, lines 298–301)

One of the quotations listed above is very close in meaning and tone to one of the most famous pronouncements on the theme in English literature, by Falstaff in William Shakespeare's play *Henry IV Part I*:

> What is honour? A word. What is in that word? Honour. What is that honour? Air. Who hath it? He that died on Wednesday. Doth he feel it? No. Doth he hear it? No. 'Tis insensible [cannot be felt] then? Yea, to the dead. But will it not live with the living? No. Why? Detraction [abuse by others] will not suffer it. Therefore, I'll none of it.
>
> (Act V, Scene I, lines 134–140)

✦ *Activity*

a See if you can identify in each case in the above list:
- the speaker
- how the word 'honour' is being used.

b What does the frequency and use made of the word 'honour' suggest to you about:
- its role in Restoration society?
- Wycherley's presentation of the theme in *The Country Wife*?

Who reads *The Country Wife*?
How do they interpret it?

A number of Restoration plays, including *The Country Wife*, were popular with audiences and critics well into the eighteenth century, but then, suddenly, they virtually disappeared from production for nearly 200 years. Criticism of the genre ranged from the moral:

> ... too filthy to handle and too noisome even to approach
> (Lord Macaulay in 1841)

to the artistic:

> Nobody with any sense of the theatre would employ the aside
> as clumsily as Wycherley in *The Plain Dealer*
> (Harley Granville Barker in 1930)

However, in general by the late nineteenth century, a more positive view was beginning to emerge. Edmund Gosse, writing in 1889, said of Wycherley that:

> ... his comedies contain very rigorous writing, much genuine wit and sound satire of the fools and rogues the author saw about him.

Algernon Swinburne, in 1895, described William Congreve as

> the greatest English master of pure comedy

and his most famous play *The Way of the World* as

> ... the unequalled and unapproached masterpiece of English Comedy.

In the present century there has been renewed interest in, and respect for, Restoration comedy, and *The Country Wife*, the most revived of all the plays, has attracted particular interest. Modern critics have seen Wycherley as a remarkably perceptive social analyst:

Extract 1

Wycherley made himself a master of the genre, and adapted it
to his own more trenchant view of the world. Coarse, savage,
obscene, he often equivocates between manners and morals,
and was deeply influenced by Molière, especially in his two
outstanding works, *The Country Wife* and *The Plain Dealer*,
both produced in the mid-1670s. In these plays he is
preoccupied with sexual desire at its most coarse and direct, yet
cannot conceal his objections to the new permissiveness and to
the current standards of behaviour, both male and female.
'Lord,' says his Lady Fidget in *The Country Wife*, 'why should
you not think that we women make use of our reputation, as
you men of yours, only to deceive the world with less
suspicion? Our virtue is like the statesman's religion, the
quaker's word, the gamester's oath and the great man's
honour, but to cheat those who trust us.' Wycherley never quite
moves wholeheartedly into the comedy of manners: he cannot
make himself airy and buoyant enough, and stands a little
outside, refusing to keep a sense of disappointment and
disapproval from darkening his plays.

(Ronald Harwood, *All The World's a Stage*, 1984)

Extract 2

The Country Wife is beautifully constructed and often superbly
funny. The contrast between the country wife's marriage, based
on obsessional jealousy, and the Alithea–Sparkish relationship,
based on total indifference, is skilfully pointed and the 'china
scene' is justly famous for raising innuendo to a fine art; in this
it only concentrates one of the main linguistic features of the
play, appropriately enough, since the contrast between surface
and meaning is what the play is all about. The central figure of
Horner is less a character than a powerfully personified
principle or set of related principles – rapacity, ruthlessness,
eroticism – all expressed in his resolute pursuit of sex. He is
more like Volpone than like any other Restoration gallant. The
foolishness of husbands like Sir Jaspar who put 'business'
(idling about the fringes of Whitehall) before everything else is
mocked, as is the vacuous concern of Sparkish to be thought a

true gallant, but the real venom in the play is directed against the ladies of fashion, Dainty, Fidget and Squeamish as well as against the lapsed lecher, Pinchwife. The 'china' scene is uproariously funny, but the laughter it arouses is of a peculiarly savage kind, both a celebration and an excoriation of human animality. The scene in which Pinchwife makes Margery write a letter at his dictation brings brutality very near the surface of the action, though it is frequently not far below.

(Gamini Salgado: *English Drama: A Critical Introduction*, 1980)

✦ *Activities*

1a What aspects of *The Country Wife* have the two critics quoted above found especially significant?

 b How does this correspond with your own experience of reading the text?

2 At various points in the play, issues of gender are brought into sharp focus and the female characters, in particular, can be seen in very different ways by twentieth-century readers or audiences. Find evidence in *The Country Wife* to support two alternative views that:
  • the play presents women as at least the equals of men?
  • the play presents women as subservient to men?
  This might provide an appropriate opportunity for a formal debate using the text as evidence for both points of view.

3 Why do you think that *The Country Wife* has proved so popular with twentieth-century audiences, particularly in the last 20 years?

4 Unlike revivals of other period plays, notably those of William Shakespeare, recent productions of *The Country Wife* have generally not used modern or alternative period dress/design.

 a Why do you think this is?

 b If you were going to design a modern-dress version of the play, how would you do it? Remember that the usual convention in such productions is to find modern equivalents

284

in terms of location, costume and character type. Write detailed notes on your ideas.

5 Perhaps a little surprisingly, *The Country Wife* has never been commercially filmed. Design a storyboard of a trailer for a film version. A storyboard involves depicting each camera shot or image in sequence, together with ideas about dialogue, music and sound effects at that moment. For example:

SHOT 1: A close-up from behind of a man wearing period wig. Sounds of raucous laughter interspersed with Restoration chamber music. The camera then swings around to reveal a handsome face. The shot opens up to reveal that the man (Horner) is seated in a coffee house with two similarly attired companions (Harcourt and Dorilant). A serving wench arrives with another bottle of wine (several empty ones are already on the table). The men leer seductively at her and as she goes, one of them pinches her bottom much to the delight of the others. A voiceover announces 'London 1675 – a time of pleasure'.

You need to bear in mind what sort of audience you would be aiming to attract and how you feel that the play can best be marketed to exploit its most appealing features. Accompany your work with a set of notes justifying your decisions.

6 Imagine that you are the manager of a modern theatre which is putting on a production of *The Country Wife* and you receive from a member of the public the letter shown on the next page.

Write a response to this letter in which you defend your decision to put on the play. Try to ensure your reply refers to as many as possible of the specific points raised, as well as attempting to defend the play's artistic integrity and worth as a whole.

◆

Dear Madam/Sir

I recently had the misfortune to attend a performance of what I can only describe as one of the most shocking examples of so-called art I have ever witnessed. I refer, of course, to your revival of William Wycherley's play 'The Country Wife' which, in my view, would have been better left to gather dust on some forgotten library shelf.

At a time when we are trying to encourage our young people to take a more responsible attitude towards personal conduct in general, and sexual matters in particular, what value can there be in showing a set of idle wastrels with more money than sense devote their whole lives to the pursuit of self-gratification? Most of the characters seem to have little else upon their minds but money or sex and in one or two particularly outrageous instances, such as the scene with the china, the way in which their physical desires are presented has gone well beyond the boundaries of good taste.

I am particularly concerned about the message that will be taken up by the impressionable regarding the portrayal of Horner and Margery. Horner is I, suppose, the hero (if that term is applicable in this play) and his phlegmatic, single-minded and successful plan paints immorality and irresponsibility in a very positive and attractive light. In the case of Margery, we see an innocent young girl corrupted before our very eyes and by the end, when she lies to cover up the truth of her liaison with Horner, she has embraced the same standards of depravity as the rest of the squalid bunch. In doing so, the sanctity of marriage is explicitly desecrated and mocked.

I would urge you to consider withdrawing the play from your repertoire at the earliest opportunity and I trust that you will choose 'period' plays in the future which are morally edifying and do have something useful to say to modern audiences.

Yours faithfully

Mr O F Fended

PS Can I recommend 'Romeo and Juliet' as a suitable play for the young?

FURTHER READING

Other Restoration comedies

Only a fraction of the plays written in the Restoration are generally available in print. However, if you are able to obtain them, the following are all worth reading and make interesting comparisons with *The Country Wife*:

William Congreve *Love for Love* (1695)

The Way of the World (1700)

George Etherege *The Man of Mode* (1676)

George Farquhar *The Recruiting Officer* (1706)

The Beaux' Stratagem (1707)

Sir John Vanbrugh *The Relapse* (1696)

The Provoked Wife (1697)

William Wycherley *The Plain Dealer* (1676)

Background Reading

R. W. Bevis, *English Drama: Restoration and Eighteenth Century* (Longman, 1988)

John Russell Brown and Bernard Harris (eds), *Restoration Theatre* (Arnold, 1965)

Donald Bruce, *Topics in Restoration Comedy* (Gollancz, 1974)

F. J. Burford, *Wits, Wenches and Wantons* (Robert Hale, 1986)

Edward Burns, *Restoration Comedy: Crises of Desire and Identity* (Macmillan, 1987)

Bonamy Dobree, *Restoration Comedy, 1660–1720* (Oxford University Press, 1924)

Ronald Harwood, *All the World's a Stage* (BBC Publications, 1984)

Elizabeth Howe, *The First English Actresses* (Cambridge University Press, 1992)

R. Leacroft, *The Development of the English Playhouse* (Methuen, 1973)

R. Loftis, *Restoration Drama: Modern Essays in Criticism* (Oxford University Press, 1966)

E. Miner (ed.), *Restoration Dramatists: A Collection of Critical Essays* (Prentice-Hall, 1966)

Gamini Salgado, *English Drama: A Critical Introduction* (Arnold, 1980)

J. L. Styan, *Restoration Comedy in Performance* (Cambridge University Press, 1986)